A Practical Guide to Staff Development:

Tools and techniques for effective education

Adrianne E. Avillion, DEd, RN

A Practical Guide to Staff Development: Tools and techniques for effective education
is published by HCPro, Inc.

Copyright 2004 HCPro, Inc.

HCPro provides information resources for the healthcare industry. A selected listing of
other newsletters and books is found in the back of this book.

HCPro is not affiliated in any way with the Joint Commission on Accreditation of
Healthcare Organizations, which owns the JCAHO trademark.

Adrianne E. Avillion, DEd, RN, Author
John Gettings, Associate Editor
Jean St. Pierre, Creative Director
Jackie Diehl Singer, Graphic Artist
Steve DeGrappo, Cover Designer
Kathy Levesque, Group Publisher
Suzanne Perney, Publisher

Advice given is general. Readers should consult professional counsel for specific legal, ethical, or clinical questions.

Arrangements can be made for quantity discounts.

For more information, contact:

HCPro, Inc.
200 Hoods Lane
P.O. Box 1168
Marblehead, MA 01945
Telephone: 800/650-6787 or 781/639-1872
Fax: 781/639-2982
E-mail: *customerservice@hcpro.com*

Visit HCPro at its World Wide Web sites:
www.hcpro.com and www.hcmarketplace.com.

6/2004
19535

TABLE OF CONTENTS

LIST OF FIGURES

ABOUT THE AUTHOR

Adrianne E. Avillion, DEd, RN

Adrianne E. Avillion, DEd, RN, is the president and owner of AEA Consulting in York, PA. She specializes in designing continuing education programs for healthcare professionals and freelance medical writing. She also offers consulting services in work redesign, quality improvement, and staff development.

Avillion has published extensively, including serving as editor of the first and second editions of *The Core Curriculum for Staff Development.* She is also a frequent presenter at conferences and conventions devoted to continuing education and staff development. She was recently elected vice president of the board of directors for the National Nursing Staff Development Organization. Avillion holds a master's degree in nursing and a doctorate in adult education from Penn State University.

INTRODUCTION

As I reflect on the constantly changing healthcare environment, I cannot help but be struck by the increasing demands such changes have placed on staff-development specialists. Practice is no longer limited to specific departments, but has expanded, in many instances, to include responsibility for entire hospitals and health systems. The rapidity with which advances in medical diagnosis, treatment, and technology are taking place makes continuing education for healthcare personnel more critical than ever before.

This book is designed to offer practical information for the successful creation of staff development products and services. It is divided five units:

- Foundations of staff development
- Teaching adults
- Teaching strategies for adults
- Addressing specific staff-development challenges
- Assessing the effectiveness of education

This book is a resource for people new to staff development as well as those who are more experienced. It is intended to help the reader identify trends and deal with current challenges:

- Addressing various learning styles
- Teaching multigenerational audiences
- Incorporating distance learning methodology
- Documenting educational effectiveness (including ROI)

This book also provides templates and tools for developing your own programs. These templates and tools are included on the CD-ROM included in this book.

UNIT 1

Foundations of staff development

Chapter 1

Evolution of staff development

Staff development is the process of providing continuing education and training for people who work in organizations that specialize in the delivery of healthcare products and services. Historically, staff-development departments were staffed by nurses for the purpose of conducting orientation and on-the-job training for members of the nursing department. Today, however, staff-development departments are staffed by a variety of disciplines and are often responsible for the delivery of training products and services to entire hospitals and healthcare systems.

Its origin

Nursing staff development began with Florence Nightingale's efforts to establish training schools for nurses and to improve the efficiency of care delivery in hospitals. Nightingale encouraged nurses to embark on a journey of life-long learning and to use their knowledge to improve patient care. However, there were few formal staff-development programs for nurses in the late 1800s and early 1900s.

The Great Depression of the late 1920s and 1930s forced many nurses into the hospital setting for the first time since their initial training. Prior to the Depression, most nurses earned their living as private-duty nurses in private practice, and nursing students provided the majority of care to hospitalized patients. However, the Depression drastically decreased the number of people who could afford private care. Hospital administrators found themselves hiring graduate nurses to work in the hospital.

This shift in practice triggered the need for various types of staff-development services. Newly hired nurses required orientation to hospital routines, procedures, policies, equipment, and regulations. These nurses had to learn to function as members of a team that cared for large numbers of patients rather than as individual practitioners who had only one patient at a time. Educational emphasis was on orientation to the hospital setting and inservice training for on-the-job skills.

The advent of World War II brought even more changes to the profession. Nurses left hospitals in large numbers to join the armed forces, causing a shortage of active nurses at home. The number of nonprofessional staff increased in an effort to compensate for the lack of registered nurses. Refresher courses for inactive nurses returning to hospital work became part of staff-development responsibilities. Training, inservice, and continuing education for nonprofessional staff added to the services provided by staff-development specialists.

In the 1940s and 1950s nurses and other healthcare personnel began to evaluate their responsibilities and necessary qualifications against standards being set by various professional organizations. In 1953, the Joint Commission for the Improvement of Care of the Patient proposed that a distinct department devoted to the training and continuing education of the nursing department be established. Leadership and management training became part of the staff-development role in the 1960s as the need for administrative skills became more apparent. The need for an objective, scientific evaluation of nursing care delivery against documented standards of quality became important not only for the well-being of patients, but also to establish how and why nursing is practiced. In 1969, the Medical College of Virginia's Health Sciences Division of Virginia Commonwealth University sponsored the first national conference on continuing education for nurses.

Specialty status

Several critical events pertaining to the establishment of staff development as a distinct healthcare specialty occurred in the 1970s:

- 1970: *The Journal of Continuing Education in Nursing* was published

- 1973: The American Nurses' Association (ANA) established the Council on Continuing Education

- 1974: *The Process of Staff Development: Components for Change* was published, which defined the practice of staff development until the 1980s

- 1978: The ANA published *Guidelines for Staff Development*

- 1978: The Join Commission on Accreditation of Hospitals mandated that a position to oversee and coordinate staff development activities be established in its affiliated hospitals

A part of the business plan

The viewpoint that healthcare is truly a business was acknowledged by both healthcare personnel and consumers during the 1980s. The need for education pertaining to financial management and the business aspects of healthcare became essential as the industry moved toward the for-profit sector. The following 1980s events show that staff development was increasingly being viewed as both a necessity and a specialty within the healthcare arena:

- 1985: *The Journal of Nursing Staff Development* (now known as the *Journal for Nurses in Staff Development)* was published.

- 1989: The National Nursing Staff Development Organization (NNSDO) was established

- Several books devoted to the practice of nursing staff-development were published

Credentialing

During the 1990s rapid advances in technology and the prevention and treatment of disease triggered the need for life-long learning among all who work in the healthcare field. These advances also clarified the need for properly credentialled, experienced staff-development specialists. Highlights of the 1990s include the following:

- 1992: The ANA published *Roles and Responsibilities for Nursing continuing Education and Staff Development Across All Settings*

- 1992: The American Nurses Credentialing Center offered the first certification examination for nursing continuing education and staff development

- 1995: The first *Core Curriculum for Nursing Staff Development* was published

- Many staff-development departments' responsibilities expanded to include the provision of education for entire hospitals and health systems, including multisite organizations

- Emphasis shifted from provision of services to evaluating how education affects organizational effectiveness

- The term "staff development" was replaced in some organizations with other terms such as "organizational development," "corporate university," "education department," and "professional-development department."

- Qualifications for leadership in staff development focused on educational and managerial expertise rather than clinical expertise

Today and beyond

The 21st century brings a new era of challenges and excitement for staff-development specialists. Nursing shortages occur with frightening regularity. But despite such shortages, healthcare professionals are expected to provide safe and appropriate care. Let's look at some of the most obvious changes by comparing traditional staff-development services to those of 2004 and beyond.

Then: In the late 1970s, physical assessment skills (e.g., heart and lung auscultation) were new, trendy topics. Continuing education classes focused on the acquisition and development of these skills.
Now: These skills are the norm, not the exception.

Then: Clinical expertise was once the primary criterion to leadership promotion.
Now: Clinical expertise has been replaced with the need for strong administrative, financial, and leadership skills.

Then: Twenty years ago, most inservice and continuing education offerings were held during the day in formal classroom settings.

Now: Education is offered around the clock, often via distance-learning techniques such as computer-based learning (CBL) and self-learning activities.

Then: The burden of responsibility for learning was placed on staff-development specialists. They were accountable for the willingness (or lack thereof) of the learners to learn.

Now: The burden has switched to healthcare professionals. There is greater emphasis on life-long learning.

Then: As recently as the 1980s, education evaluation focused on the number of participants who attended a program, learner satisfaction, and the number of programs offered monthly.

Now: Educators must look at the "big picture." In other words, how does the provision of education affect organizational performance?

Then: The staff-development specialist's role was once solely that of educator.

Now: Staff-development specialists assume multiple roles, including researcher, consultant, change agent, manager, and performance coach, in addition to educator.

Then: Traditionally, staff-development specialists' teaching skills focused on classroom learning.

Now: They are expected to be experts in a variety of teaching methods, particularly distance learning and CBL.

As healthcare evolves and changes, so do the roles and responsibilities of staff-development specialists. The only certainty in healthcare is that change is, and will continue to be, constant. Staff-development specialists must be experts in adaptation and provide educational resources to ensure that the quality of patient care remains safe, appropriate, and of high quality.

To meet this challenge, staff-development departments must establish sound operational foundations. The basis of such foundations is the development of practical mission, vision, and values statements and corresponding goals.

References

Avillion, A. E. (1998). *The redesign of nursing staff development.* Pensacola, FL: The National Nursing Staff Development Organization (NNSDO).

Brunt, B. A., Pack, J. T., and Parr, P. (2001). *The history of staff development.* In A. E. Avillion (Ed.), Core curriculum for staff development (2nd ed.) (pp. 3–17). Pensacola, FL: NNSDO.

DeSilets, L. D., and Pinkerton, S. E. (2004). "Looking back on 25 years of continuing education." *The Journal of Continuing Education in Nursing,* 35(1), pp. 12–13.

Nightingale, F. (1859). *Notes on nursing.* London: Harrison and Sons.

Tobin, H. M., Yoder, P. S., Hull, P. K., and Scott, B. C. (1974). *The process of staff development. Components for change.* St. Louis: Mosby.

Chapter 2

Values, vision, mission, and goals

Do you think mission, vision, and values statements are important? Do they guide your staff-development practice? Do you consider them just a "paper exercise"? If you answered "yes" to the last question, then the information in this section is especially necessary for you to understand.

The staff-development mission, vision, and values statements establish a foundation for the delivery of education. You must write statements that appropriately guide the way you deliver your department's products and services.

This section will define the terms values, vision, and mission. Templates to help you write practical, usable statements are also provided. Finally, recommendations are included to help you write corresponding goals.

Values

A values statement (referred to as a philosophy by some organizations) is a set of beliefs and principles that guide your department's activities to achieve a specific purpose. These values must be stated clearly and succinctly and should guide your department's response when unexpected challenges arise. All members of the staff-development department must understand and agree with identified values.

Sample values statement

FIGURE 2.1

Staff Development Department of Community Health System

Our primary responsibility as staff-development specialists is to offer the employees of Community Health System education programs that enhance their abilities to establish and maintain a safe and appropriate environment for the delivery of high-quality patient care.

We respect the dignity, individuality, and cultural beliefs of all learners. We must provide valid and reliable education activities that meet the needs of our learners. We use various teaching/learning methods including, but not limited to, classroom learning, computer-based learning, self-learning initiatives, and other forms of distance education.

The staff development department of Community Health System adheres to the following standards:

- Learning is a lifelong process.

- Adults are self-directed learners.

- Teaching/learning is a dynamic, interactive process between the learner and the staff-development specialist conducted in an environment of mutual respect and regard.

- Adult learners bring a wealth of life experiences to any teaching/learning situation. These experiences facilitate the teaching/learning experience.

The staff development specialist is responsible for

- identifying the educational needs of the organization

- planning education programs based on identified needs of the learners for the purpose of enhancing organizational effectiveness

- creating education programs that meet the needs of the learners

- evaluating the effectiveness of education programs as measured by their effect on organizational effectiveness

- using evaluation data to improve educational activities

Sample values statement (cont.)

FIGURE 2.1

Learners are responsible for

- identifying their education needs
- achieving their education goals
- attending relevant/necessary education programs
- maintaining competence
- contributing to the success of education programs
- evaluating the effectiveness of education programs
- assuming responsibility for his or her life-long learning

Organizational leadership is responsible for

- supporting an environment that facilitates life-long learning
- collaborating with the staff-development department to achieve the organization's education goals
- facilitating learners' ability to participate in education activities
- attending relevant or necessary education programs
- participating in the evaluation of education's impact on organizational effectiveness

A values statement like the one in Figure 2.1 can be written only in conjunction with the organization's values statement. When writing your values statement, make sure you have a copy of your organization's values statement in front of you. If administration does not agree and overtly support staff-development values, you will find it difficult, if not impossible, to achieve your goals and objectives.

In fact, two of the top reasons education fails are due to administration:

1. Lack of commitment to and involvement with the education process

2. Failure to hold participants accountable for their own learning

Include language in your statement that addresses these issues; it is integral. Unfortunately, most staff-developments specialists experience both factors at some point during their careers. Therefore, work closely with administrators and managers when developing your values statement. If you cannot agree on values, consider finding employment within another organization—one whose values coincide with yours.

Vision

Your vision is an image of what you want your department's future to be. It must be precise, easily understood, and well-written. Your vision must be clear not only to those within the staff-development department, but to those who use your products and services. Your vision should pull the staff-development department together as employees strive to build a common identity and future. A well-crafted vision statement is

- driven by your values
- future-oriented
- realistic
- inspiring
- concise

Sample vision statement #1

FIGURE 2.2

Children's City Hospital Staff-Development Department

It is the vision of the Staff-Development Department to be a statewide leader in the provision of education programs that focus on excellence in pediatric healthcare services.

Sample vision statement #2

FIGURE 2.3

American Rehabilitation System Education Department

It is the vision of the Education Department of the American Rehabilitation System to be a national leader of professional staff development and continuing education dedicated to excellence in physical medicine and rehabilitation products and services.

Visions must be realistic. A vision that has national implications is probably not achievable if you work in a small community hospital. A vision should inspire staff to work to their maximum abilities, but must also be attainable. A vision that is unrealistic will discourage more than it motivates.

Recommendations for crafting a vision

FIGURE 2.4

1. Determine the department's strengths and weaknesses.

2. Determine what is inspirational and what is realistic.

3. When writing your vision, consider the following questions:

   - What does the organization expect education and training to accomplish?

   - What does the staff-development department expect education and training to accomplish?

   - How does the staff-development department contribute to the quality and appropriateness of patient care?

   - How does the staff-development department support the organization's financial plan?

   - Does this vision complement the values of the staff-development department and the organization?

   - Does this vision stem from your organizational vision?

4. Incorporate your vision statement in all departmental activities, including but not limited to needs assessments, program planning and implementation, quality improvement activities, and performance evaluations.

5. Evaluate your vision statement regularly.

Mission

The mission must clearly communicate the purpose and direction of staff-development activities to persons within and outside of the department. It describes essential functions as well as the overall reason for the department's existence.

Sample mission statement

FIGURE 2.5

The staff-development department of the Hazlewood Healthcare System upholds the mission, vision, and values of the organization by developing and offering educational products and services crafted to improve the quality and appropriateness of patient care.

Educational products and services enhance organizational effectiveness by providing programming designed to increase knowledge and skills of employees. The staff development department facilitates the maintenance of Commission on Accreditation of Rehabilitation Facilities (CARF) standards for the organization's five freestanding physical-medicine and rehabilitation hospitals by designing products and services specific to the needs of rehabilitation staff.

The mission statement in Figure 2.5 obviously focuses on an area of great organizational importance: Its five freestanding rehabilitation facilities. If something is important to your organization, it is important to you. Do not write a mission statement that conflicts with your organization's mission.

Suppose your organization has recently purchased several long-term care facilities. You are excited about the possibility of developing education for staff who work with a geriatric population; however, your administration has decided to outsource educational activities for these new acquisitions and wants you to concentrate on facilitating trauma-center accreditation at various sites within the system. In fact, your organization's vision is to become a national leader in trauma care. No matter how much you believe that long-term care education should be a priority for your department, emphasizing this in your mission or values is a mistake because it conflicts with organizational emphasis.

Use the characteristics of a mission statement detailed in Figure 2.6 when you sit down to write your mission statement.

FIGURE 2.6

Characteristics of a mission statement

The mission statement must

- reflect departmental and organizational values and vision

- reflect—never contradict—the organization's mission

- identify what the staff-development department does for the organization

- focus on both organizational and departmental priorities

- serve as the foundation for departmental goals and objectives

- be reviewed regularly and revised as organizational priorities evolve and change

Goals

Goals are broadly written statements that identify what the staff-development department should accomplish within a specified period of time. They interpret the mission statement as the intentions that direct the department's activities. Departmental goals must be based on relevant organizational goals. They should link the provision of education and organizational business goals. The plan to achieve each goal consists of measurable, realistic objectives. Objectives must identify who is responsible for their achievement and within what time frame the objectives must be achieved. Objectives guide the delegation of work within the department.

Let's return to the mission statement in Figure 2.5 from the fictitious Hazlewood Healthcare System and develop a goal and objectives based on this mission.

Sample goal and corresponding objectives

FIGURE 2.7

Goal: Achieve CARF accreditation for freestanding physical rehabilitation facilities within Hazlewood Healthcare System.

Objective	Responsibility	Deadline
1. Review CARF standards pertaining to education and summarize them for staff-development department and the managers and staff of the rehabilitation facilities.	S. Sanders, RN, MEd P. Davis, PT, MEd	10/14/2005
2. Delegate responsibility for specific education activities at identified rehabilitation facilities.	A. Mendel, RN, DEd, Director, staff development	10/14/2005
3. Evaluate current adherence to CARF education standards and formulate action plan to improve/maintain adherence.	A. Mendel, RN, DEd, S. Sanders, RN, MEd P. Davis, PT, MEd	10/31/2005

Notice that the goals in Figure 2.7 stem from both organizational priorities and the departmental mission statement. The objectives are measurable, identify person(s) responsible, and a deadline for achievement.

The mission, vision, values, and goal statements are the foundations of your staff-development department's practice. As you think about your own statements, consider the trends that now, or will in the future, affect how your department functions.

References

Avillion, A. E. (2003). *Writing a staff development plan: business strategies for the 21st century.* Pensacola, FL: The National Nursing Staff Development Organization (NNSDO).

Brunt, B. A. (2001). "Philosophy, mission, and goals." In A. E. Avillion (Ed.), *Core curriculum for staff development* (2nd ed.) (pp. 19-30). Pensacola, FL: NNSDO.

Phillips, J. J., and Phillips, P. P. (2002). "Reasons why training & development fails and what you can do about it." *Training,* 39(9), pp. 78–85.

Tiffany, P., and Peterson, S. D. (1997). *Business plans for dummies.* Foster City, CA: IDG Books.

Chapter 3

Current trends in staff development

Education is one of the most effective tools for performance improvement and helping staff to deal with the constantly changing healthcare environment. Following are some trends to avoid. Some already affect how you function as a staff-development specialist; Others will affect you soon. Think about these trends as you build the foundation of your plan.

Business strategies and financial issues

Education products and services must be aligned with your organization's business strategy. Your ability to objectively document staff development's effect on the organization's financial stability is critical. Because all departments must be able to document such impact, education pertaining to business strategies and financial issues will be a high priority for your department—if it is not already.

Leadership and management skills for the next generation

The first group of baby boomers turns 65 years old in 2011. As they and their fellow boomers leave the work force, it is anticipated that job vacancies will outnumber available workers by 4.3 million. Healthcare, already feeling the strain of significant personnel shortages, will need educated, skilled workers in great numbers. These conditions will make it more important than ever to have highly qualified leaders in the healthcare arena.

Soft skills

Training and education on so-called "soft skills" are a top priority now and will continue to be in the future. These skills are closely related to any organization's business goals and objectives: how patients and other customers are treated; the ability to communicate; dealing with workplace violence; recognizing, preventing, and coping with sexual harassment; and enhancing understanding among cultures contribute to the success—or failure—of all businesses, including healthcare.

Distance learning

The need for distance education will increase, and the need for classroom education will decrease. Classroom learning will always have a place in the staff-development arena, but the generations who are now, or will soon be, entering the work force are accustomed to all types of distance education and expect education and training to be offered at convenient times and places. Telecommuting has become increasingly popular. You must meet the needs of employees who spend significant amounts of time away from the organization's physical location but are connected to the organization virtually.

Accelerated learning

Rapid advances in technology and the prevention, diagnosis, and treatment of injury and illness require almost daily updates and extensive continuing education. With the retirement of the baby boomer generation, orientation of new healthcare employees must be conducted at frequent, time-efficient intervals. This means that accelerated teaching/learning will be an essential staff-development technique in the 21st century. The ability to teach creatively while enhancing learning at a rapid rate is the crux of accelerated learning. Accelerated learning's foundation is the same as adult learning—teaching/learning activities are viewed as dynamic, interactive collaborations with an emphasis on activity-centered learning.

Scope of practice

As staff-development responsibilities increase and the scope of practice widens, the name of your department and the titles of your staff may change to reflect these factors.

Examples of department names include, but are not limited to, education services, professional development, corporate university, center for learning, center for excellence, human resources (HR) effectiveness, and organizational development.

These are trends you need to deal with effectively. They will also affect the qualifications for those who work as staff-development specialists and the roles they play within an organization.

A culture of learning

FIGURE 3.1

Organizations are beginning to understand the value of establishing a culture of learning. An organization that supports a culture of learning believes that education is essential for the professional development of all employees and for the continued improvement of patient-care services. There is an atmosphere of internal trust among administration, management, and staff that encourages open sharing of knowledge and skills. Integral to the philosophy, values, mission, and vision is a strong belief that education, learning, and knowledge management are essential components of organizational effectiveness. Organizational leaders are visionaries and use knowledge, learning, and education to facilitate organizational growth. Also, within this culture

- senior administration and middle management
    - highly value and are extremely supportive of education
    - respect those responsible for the coordination and delivery of education products and services
    - facilitate employees' attendance at learning activities

- employees
    - understand they are responsible for continuing education and professional development and seek out learning activities at every available opportunity

- the entire organization
    - supports the evaluation of learning activities at all levels of evaluation
    - embraces change and is able to adapt to emerging patient and employee needs
    - is responsive to the concerns of its employees and values their input

References

Hall, B., and Boehle, S. (2004). "Top training priorities for 2004: The second annual leaders of learning survey." *Training,* 41(2), pp. 26–33.

Meier, D. (2000). *The accelerated learning handbook.* New York: McGraw-Hill.

Chapter 4

Qualifications for the staff-development specialist

Staff-development specialists carry a great deal of responsibility and must be highly skilled educators and leaders. The ideal candidate has a graduate degree in the adult-education field and significant experience as a staff-development specialist in the healthcare arena. However, education and experience do not necessarily mean these people are excellent teachers—and they need to be.

As part of the decision-making process, ask candidates to develop and carry out an adult-education program for some of your organization's employees. Keep it simple—you don't want them to spend too much time and effort working on a project and then not hire them. Select a learning activity that is relatively easy to implement and give them some guidance about why this program is important to the organization. This will give you a chance to observe their program-planning skills and teaching ability. Ask them to present a proposal for evaluating the effectiveness of their programs as well.

Your departmental clinical and nonclinical educators should demonstrate clinical expertise and leadership qualities. They should also have a talent for and interest in the education process. In conjunction with their department managers, you can groom potential educators. Help them develop adult-education, program-planning, and teaching skills and train them in the evaluation process. Consider offering learning activities that deal with teaching skills and education planning. Most clinical employees are responsible for some aspect of patient education and would benefit from such learning activities even if they never want to become educators. You may recognize potential educators during such programs and then determine their interest in educator roles.

What happens when there is not an abundance of candidates for staff-development positions? Suppose the only available candidates are clinical educators?

Use these tips to select clinical and nonclinical educators to groom as staff-development specialists.

- **Determine basic education requirements.** A background or the pursuit of a background in adult education is essential. Make this a requirement. If you want to groom someone without this background, require that they achieve either a degree or certificate in adult education within a specified time period and demonstrate their active pursuit of this goal regularly.

- **Discover who your teachers are.** Remember that expertise in a noneducator role does not mean that someone will automatically be a good teacher. The most experienced, excellent nurse may not be able to adequately communicate their knowledge. Effective teaching is an art and a talent.

- **Observe and assess candidates in action.** Interested candidates should plan and carry out an education program with your assistance. They will need more help than a staff-development candidate with educator experience. This will not only give you an opportunity to observe their education skills, but also to assess how eager they are to pursue the staff-development role.

Orientation

Have you though about how you will orient new staff-development specialists? Many persons involved in healthcare-learning activities forget they must provide a well-developed orientation for those new to the staff-development department. Following are components of a staff-development orientation program:

- Practical implementation of the principles of adult learning

- Recognition of various learning styles and teaching methodologies for each style

- Differentiation of the characteristics of various generations in the workplace and preferred teaching/learning styles of each generation

- How to conduct needs assessments and analyze collected data

- How to plan and implement education programs based on needs-assessment data, organizational priorities, quality-improvement findings, and accreditation standards

- Recognition of the five levels of program evaluation and how to conduct an evaluation at each level

- Identifying techniques that motivate adult learners

- How to plan, implement, and evaluate distance-learning activities

- How to implement resourceful teaching strategies

You'll probably think of more issues that will eventually become part of your staff-development competency program. Education employees must demonstrate that they are competent to fulfill the various roles within your department. A good orientation is the foundation of a new educator's success.

Crafting a job description

The qualifications necessary for being a staff educator depend on the roles and responsibilities of the department. Look at your organization's mission, vision, and values. Where does education fit into the organizational plan? Before you can determine qualifications and subsequent job descriptions, answer the following questions:

- Do you work in a single hospital or a system that consists of several hospitals/healthcare facilities (e.g., long-term care, hospice, or outpatient clinics)?

- If you work in a healthcare system, who is responsible for education endeavors? Does each facility within the system have a distinct staff-development department that functions autonomously or is responsibility centralized? Are staff-development specialists expected to provide education for multiple sites?

- Does the staff-development department consist of both full- and part-time staff?

- Who is responsible for the administrative management of education? Does this position also have direct responsibility for program planning?

- Do some staff members function in dual roles of staff-development specialist and direct patient-care provider?

- What value does the organization place on education? How does the organization express this in its mission, vision, and values statements?

There are countless ways to determine staff-development qualifications because there are countless ways to craft the various roles and responsibilities. Qualifications are and must remain essential components of job descriptions. Here are some guidelines to follow when determining qualifications and translating them into appropriate job descriptions

Job title

The job title should reflect the position's scope of responsibility. For example, "vice-president for education" may be an appropriate title for someone in charge of education for a large health system. But if you are responsible for education services for a large nursing department, "director of staff development for nursing services" may best reflect your role.

Qualifications

First determine whether specific licensure is required. Decide whether a specific amount and type of clinical expertise is necessary. This may be especially important for staff who function primarily as clinical educators or who have responsibility for particular clinical disciplines.

Graduate education is rapidly becoming the norm for persons holding responsibility for large, systemwide departments. Some large health systems are now looking for doctorally prepared candidates for vice president or director positions. Specific education qualifications will depend on specific roles and responsibilities. For example, a vice-president for education or director of staff development needs managerial qualifications, including business expertise, in addition to qualifications in education. Clinical expertise is not essential. In fact, clinical staff-development specialists may find themselves reporting to someone who has graduate degrees in business or education, but no clinical background.

If you find an ideal candidate who is currently working on a required graduate degree, allow that person a specific amount of time to complete his or her education and hire him or her anyway. Be specific about length and type of experience needed and put it in writing and stick to it. A director role may require time as a middle manager in addition to education experience. An information systems trainer will need specific expertise as a computer specialist.

As distance learning becomes more of a necessity, add specific computer, teleconferencing, and similar skills as requirements.

General working conditions

Be as specific as possible about the hours required, including the need to work weekends, holidays, and shift work as appropriate. This is especially true if you are sharing a position with another department (e.g., a registered nurse working as a clinical educator for the staff-development department 24 hours per week and as a bedside nurse 16 hours per week).

Identify any physical demands. For example, "Must be able to lift, move, and position equipment such as classroom chairs, tables, and audiovisual equipment of at least 30 lbs on a regularly."

Identify any potential for exposure to dangerous situations, such as patients with infectious diseases or dealing with patients who are violent. List observance of specific precautions (e.g., mandatory training to deal with violence, wearing protective clothing, etc.).

Reporting mechanism

Clearly define reporting lines. If someone reports to two managers, as in the case of a shared position, make sure that this is made clear.

Summary of responsibilities

This general summary should include an overview of responsibilities including what positions, if any, this particular position supervises. It should also include a statement about ensuring that services are consistent with organizational and departmental mission, vision, values, and goals.

Major responsibilities

Be sure that the responsibilities you craft can be adequately evaluated. For example, most staff-development roles contain a statement such as, "Implements the principles of adult learning in program planning and implementation." But what exactly does this mean? How is it measured?

Include qualifiers such as, "This is measured by including learners in the program planning process," or "Encourages input from learners."

Qualifying statements should be written for each adult learning principle. Clinical positions generally have detailed descriptions of responsibilities, and so should staff-development specialists.

Add attendance at mandatory education events and how many hours of continuing education should be attained every year as part of the job responsibilities. Also, include a statement explaining that responsibilities will be assessed and modified ongoing in accordance with the needs of the organization.

Remember—change is constant!

References

Avillion, A. E. (2003). *Writing a staff development plan: business strategies for the 21st century.* Pensacola, FL: The National Nursing Staff Development Organization (NNSDO).

Fischer, K., Franck, L., and Seay, S. J. (2001). "Role of the manager in staff development." In A. E. Avillion (Ed.), *Core curriculum for staff development* (2nd ed.) (pp. 48–512). Pensacola, FL: NNSDO.

Chapter 5

Emerging roles of the staff-development specialist

As discussed earlier, staff-development specialists fulfill more roles than that of educator. The responsibilities for education are clear cut. But how prepared are you to assume one or more of the roles that have recently found their way into the staff-development arena? To help you determine your preparedness, read the following descriptions of some of these new roles and issues that coincide with their evolution.

CLO or CKO

The chief learning officer (CLO) or chief knowledge officer (CKO) is the person responsible for discerning, organizing, and documenting the collective knowledge of a healthcare organization, and he or she has the opportunity to significantly influence the evolution of the organization. This person oversees the provision of education endeavors for the organization and is instrumental in evaluating the impact of knowledge, learning, and education on the organization.

The CLO or CKO is typically a member of the senior administrative team and fulfills a strategic role. This is a new role, and to justify its existence, education's positive effect on the organization—including its financial solvency—must be objectively demonstrated.

Director of the center for excellence

Similar to the roles of the CLO or CKO, this role emphasizes education's goal to achieve excellence among an organization's employees, patients, and products and services.

Performance coach

The ability to enhance job performance is frequently viewed as part of the educator's role. The staff-development specialist who is a performance coach functions as a coach, role model, and talent developer. Coaching may be done one on one or in a group. You may be asked to coach staff, managers, physicians, administrators or any member of the organization. This role requires a great deal of tact and political savvy.

Consultant

Staff-development specialists have informally acted as consultants for many years. Recently, however, the role has become more formal. Consultations are sought in many areas, such as performance improvement, skill attainment, leadership development, and preparation for accreditation surveys. This facet of the staff-development role requires expertise in the subject matter and excellent interpersonal skills.

Researcher

Participation in clinical and quality-improvement research is often part of the staff-development specialist's role. In some health systems, nursing research falls in the realm of education services. This is most often the case in large health systems where the department director has a doctorate.

OD specialist

Organizational development (OD) focuses on providing a framework to manage an organization as a smoothly functioning system. The OD specialist's primary function is to facilitate organizationwide change while enhancing working relationships and performance improvement. These duties come naturally to the staff-development role because traditionally, educators work to improve work performance and facilitate the achievement of organizational goals.

Roles and responsibilities will continue to evolve and expand in scope and importance to the organization. Be on the alert for healthcare conditions that could trigger new roles and duties. As these roles evolve, consider what qualifications are needed to fulfill them.

References

Churley-Strom, R., and McCarthy, M. (2001). "Role of the performance coach in staff development." *Core curriculum for staff development* (2nd ed.) (pp. 561–578). Pensacola, FL: The National Nursing Staff Development Organization (NNSDO).

Donner, D. (2000). "Four facts about the new jobs of chief learning officer and chief knowledge officer." Performance in Practice (A supplement to *Training & Development Magazine*), Fall, 2000, pp. 1–2.

Stuller, J. (1998). "Chief of corporate smarts." *Training*, 35(4), pp. 28–34.

UNIT 2

Teaching adults

Chapter 6

Principles of adult learning

Nearly all staff-development specialists have a statement about the "implementation of adult-learning principles" in their job descriptions. However, when it comes to applying these principles, organizations sometimes merely give these principles lip service.

Adult-learning principles must be actively used to improve the delivery of adult education. This chapter reviews the principles of adult learning and offers recommendations for their practical implementation.

The principles

Adults need a reason for learning

Adult learners want to know why it is important for them to participate in an educational activity. Developing clear-cut objectives for an educational program is not enough. For example, suppose you have been told to implement organizationwide customer-service training. Some staff may respond by complaining, "I already know how to talk to patients. This is just a waste of time."

However, they may feel different if they knew that quality-improvement data indicate a trend in customer dissatisfaction. They need to know what complaints and concerns patients and other customers express and why it is important to address them. Staff members also need to know that customer satisfaction is the responsibility of all employees.

Communicating facts relevant to the rationale for a particular program is essential. Adults have the right as well as the responsibility to know why they are asked to acquire or maintain knowledge and skills.

Adults are self-directed learners

Adults direct their own learning. They need to feel they have some control over what they learn and how they learn it. Adults also need to feel that their learning needs are respected.

Although some training, such as Joint Commission on Accreditation of Healthcare Organizations (JCAHO)–mandated classes, is not under the direction of the learner, it is possible to offer learners choices about how they learn.

Suppose rhythm-strip interpretation is part of the orientation for newly hired nurses in the cardiac care unit. Some of these new employees may have a great deal of experience and easily interpret rhythm strips.

Offer two teaching methods: a self-learning module that, if successfully completed, allows those nurses to be exempt from the formal classroom setting, in addition to more extensive education programs. This approach allows self-direction and acknowledges existing expertise.

Adults bring a variety of life experiences to any learning situation

Life experiences enhance any learning situation. Such experiences may not directly relate to the specific topic of the program, but they can still complement learning. If you teach a program about customer service in healthcare, participants may relate stories about their own experiences in various settings from the perspective of the customer rather than the provider of services. Encourage the sharing of relevant experiences, but do not allow any one participant to dominate the discussion.

Adults focus on acquiring knowledge and skills that will help them improve their daily lives

Adults need to understand how particular knowledge and skills will benefit them as they conduct their daily activities. These benefits can be work-related or related to their personal lives. In other words, adults are task-, problem-, or life-centered in their approach to learning.

This principle correlates well with adults' need to know. You can help by including a practical rationale for learning activities and making objectives clear and measurable.

Adults are responsive to both extrinsic and intrinsic motivators

Extrinsic motivators include such factors as promotions, salary increases, better jobs, and better working conditions. Examples of intrinsic motivators are improved quality of life, enhanced job satisfaction, and increased self-esteem. Adults need to know that the knowledge and skills obtained from an activity will satisfy their extrinsic/intrinsic needs.

The following template will help you use adult-learning principles during the program planning process. It identifies specific adult-learning principles, important components of each, and space for you to customize your learning activities.

Implementing adult learning principles

FIGURE 6.1

Adult learning principle	Important considerations	Learning activity
Adults need a reason for learning	• Provide a specific rationale for the learning activity. • Make sure objectives are clear, measurable, and that the learners know what they are. • Communicate the rationale and objectives to your learners. This is especially important when an educator is not present during the learning activity (e.g., distance-learning activities).	
Adults are self-directed learners	• Adults need to feel that they have some control over what they learn and how they learn it. • Adults need to feel that their learning needs are respected.	

Implementing adult learning principles (cont.)

FIGURE 6.1

Adult learning principle	Important considerations	Learning activity
Adults bring a variety of life experiences to any learning situation	• These life experiences can enhance any learning situation. • Experiences not directly related to healthcare can be a useful part of healthcare learning activities. • Do not allow any one participant to dominate discussions at the expense of the other learners.	
Adults focus on acquiring knowledge and skills that will help them improve their daily lives	• The measurable benefits of education must be built into the rationale for learning and its objectives. • Help adult learners understand how learning activities will benefit them.	
Adults are responsive to both extrinsic and intrinsic motivators	• Motivators are linked to life improvements. • Examples of extrinsic motivators include promotions, increase in salary, and better jobs. • Examples of intrinsic factors include enhanced self-esteem, increased job satisfaction, and improved quality of life. • Adult learners need to know how learning activities will meet extrinsic and intrinsic needs.	

References

Bland, G., and Hadaway, L. C. (2001). "Principles of adult learning," *Core curriculum for staff development* (2nd ed.) (pp. 31–64). Pensacola, FL: The National Nursing Staff Development Organization (NNSDO).

Merriam, S. B., and Brockett, R. G. (1997). *The profession and practice of adult education: An introduction.* San Francisco: Jossey-Bass.

Chapter 7

Identifying learning styles

It is not enough to understand and use the principles of adult learning. You must also consider learning styles, generational differences, and cultural influences that affect how your audience retains information. This chapter deals with learning styles and how these styles affect ability to learn.

Some learners may not realize their own learning styles. If you recognize a particular style, help your learners to understand why they prefer to learn as they do. Design programs that include a variety of learning-style methods.

The learning styles

Most experts recognize three distinct styles of learning: auditory, visual, and kinesthetic. The following descriptions include the characteristics of each style, learner behaviors, and what you can do to accommodate learners of all three styles.

Auditory

Auditory learners learn predominantly by hearing. These learners prefer audiotapes, lectures, and discussions. They respond best to verbal instructions. Their preference for auditory learning is evident even in their every-day speech. They frequently make comments like, "I hear what you're saying," "I'm telling myself," and "That sounds good to me." Auditory learners often read out loud. As they speak, their brains are stimulated to assimilate knowledge and skills.

Your auditory learners will position themselves in a classroom or other learning environment so they can hear, but they don't necessarily need to have the best view of the educator. They will not enjoy numerous written handouts or visuals. This can be a particular challenge during distance-learning activities, such as computer-based learning (CBL). If possible, add auditory stimulants (e.g., instructions, verbal conversations, or music) as part of the program.

Here are some facets of the auditory-learning experience and suggestions for meeting the needs of these learners:

- Your auditory learners will reveal their emotions by changes in their tone of voice and the quality of their speech. Assess their satisfaction with the learning experience by listening to how they express themselves. They may say everything is fine, but their tone of voice tells you the opposite is true.

- These learners give excellent verbal directions and explanations.

- Auditory learners talk (aloud) through problems and procedures and expresses solutions verbally.

Visual learners

During adulthood, visual learning is the predominant learning style. Visual learners prefer to sit in the front in a classroom setting, take copious notes, and are attracted to verbal discussions that contain a lot of imagery.

These learners prefer passive surroundings and are attracted to presentations and handouts that use color, graphics, and other visual stimuli. They tend to be distracted by too much auditory stimulation. Visual learners may close their eyes to visualize what they're learning. When working with visual learners, provide visual stimulation and make sure

- handouts are well-illustrated and colorful

- the educator is easily seen in the classroom setting

- written materials are easy to read (i.e., avoid small print)

Kinesthetic learners

Kinesthetic learners learn by physical activities and direct hands-on involvement. These are the people who learn best by doing.

Kinesthetic learners need activity and cannot sit still for long periods of time. They need frequent breaks. These learners speak with their hands and display emotions through body language. They may remember what activities were performed, but have trouble remembering what they saw or what was said. These learners frequently use phrases such as, "Keep in touch," "I can't grasp this information," and "I'm following your directions." Here are suggestions for working with kinesthetic learners:

- Provide opportunities for skill demonstrations and return demonstrations.

- When directions are given, use demonstration whenever possible. This can be done in person, on videos, or during CBL.

- Provide opportunities for these learners to get up and move around.

Use the following cheat sheet to plan educational activities that include techniques suitable to all types of learners. Use the third column to customize your own learning activities.

Learning-styles cheat sheet

FIGURE 7.1

Learning style	Characteristics of the learners	Education strategies
Auditory	• Learn by hearing • In classroom setting, they need to hear, but not necessarily see, the educator • Tone of voice indicates their emotions • Use "hearing" words in their speech, such as, "I hear what you're saying," and, "That sounds right to me" • Conduct business (including learning and teaching) via the telephone with great success • Talk through problems and procedures and offer verbal solutions	• Interactive lectures and discussions • Debates • Audio/teleconferences • Audiotapes
Visual	• Sit in the front in the classroom • Take copious, detailed notes • Prefer verbal discussions that contain a lot of imagery • May close their eyes to visualize learning • Prefer illustrations and graphics that use color • Need to see what they are learning • Reveal emotions by facial expressions and pay great attention to the facial expressions of others • Prefer face-to-face learning and discussions • Eye contact is important	• Make sure that the educator is easily visible throughout the classroom • During distance learning, make sure the method (e.g., computer, video, etc.) is clear and easily seen • Use handouts, graphics, or other printed materials that are well-illustrated, well-written, and are colorful (avoid small print)

Learning-styles cheat sheet (cont.)

FIGURE 7.1

Learning style	Characteristics of the learners	Education strategies
Kinesthetic	• Need to be active (unable to sit still for long periods of time) • Prefer handling projects on a step-by-step basis • Speak with their hands • Express emotion via body language • Remember what was done, but have difficulty remembering what was said or only seen • Use phrases containing words such as "grasp," "touch," and "follow"	• Provide frequent breaks • Include opportunities for hands-on experience, such as return demonstrations • Break learning down into manageable tasks

References

Miller, S. (2000). *Three different learning styles* (Electronic version). Retrieved April 28, 2003, from *www.usd.edu/trio/tut/ts/styleres.html*.

Rose, C., and Nicholl, M. J. (1997). *Accelerated learning for the 21st century. The six-step plan to unlock your master-mind.* New York: Dell Publishing.

Chapter 8

Teaching to multigenerational audiences

Are there really differences in learning preferences among the various generations? The answer is a resounding yes! Of course, no one style or preference is common to all members of a specific generation. But generation is one of many issues to consider when planning education activities. This chapter will describe general guidelines to help you teach more effectively to multigenerational audiences.

The current work force is composed of four specific generations: veterans, baby boomers, Generation X, and Generation Net. Zemke, Raines, and Filipczak, in their 1999 article, "Generation Gaps in the Classroom," offer particularly helpful insights into teaching audiences composed of these groups.

The following descriptions identify each generation's view of the world, their beliefs about what constitutes an appealing work environment, and their preferences for how they acquire knowledge and skills. Finally, sample templates to help you plan programs for multigenerational audiences are referenced.

Veterans

The generation born between 1922 and 1943 experienced first-hand two of the most critical events of the 20th century: the Great Depression and World War II. Therefore, veterans possess experiences unique to those events that have shaped how they view themselves and the world in which they live.

Veterans are also the generation that have the most vivid memories of parents and grand-parents who came as immigrants to the United States. They possess knowledge of cultural traditions, wisdom, and wit that succeeding generations generally lack.

Veterans prefer more formal learning environments and dislike being asked to relay or listen to stories or experiences they deem too personal. As part of the formality of the learning experience, these learners expect educators to be dressed and behave in a business-like fashion. Profanity and slang should be avoided.

Veterans often view educators as authority figures, and they have been raised to respect such people. Therefore, veterans are the least likely of all learners to confront you directly if they disagree with you. You may not find out they disliked the way an activity was conducted until you read their program evaluations.

Teaching considerations

The following are tips for teaching veterans, but note that some of these points are applic-able to any adult learner:

- Make sure learning goals and objectives are clearly understood, regardless of the teaching method used. This is especially important if distance-learning techniques are used.

- When using distance learning, make it clear where veteran learners should go for help. For example, an important part of computer-based learning (CBL) is to include the educator's contact information. Will you be available for face-to-face discussion, or will you work with your learners via e-mail? Let veterans know when and where you will be available or how soon they can expect a response to an e-mail question.

- Provide organized handouts that summarize key points of the education activity.

- When developing handouts or writing CBL programs, avoid small print. Use a computer font that is easily read, such as Arial.

- Do not put veterans on the spot by asking uncomfortable questions or asking them to demonstrate unfamiliar techniques, especially in front of younger colleagues. Encourage participation in a nonthreatening way.

- Treat veterans with respect at all times.

- Establish rapport with veterans, especially if you are a younger educator. Acknowledge their life experiences, wisdom, and expertise.

- Never presume all veterans are computer illiterate.

- Never talk down to veterans.

- Motivate veterans by explaining how education will improve job performance and organizational effectiveness.

- If skill demonstration is part of the activity, allow time for practice in private.

- Since veterans are unlikely to confront you face-to-face, encourage feedback during breaks or midway through a distance-learning activity.

Baby boomers

The baby boomers are the product of the post-World War II baby boom. Born between 1944 and 1960, the boomer generation consists of an estimated 73 million people. The people of the baby boomer generation were usually doted on by their parents, and they grew up believing they were entitled to the best the world had to offer. Boomers believed it was their right and their responsibility to change the world for the better. This generation has a passionate work ethic and a desire to achieve financial success. Baby boomers invented the phrase, "Thank God it's Monday," and the 60-hour work weeks.

Baby boomers value both teamwork and personal gratification in the workplace. They are dedicated to learning and initiated the self-help book craze. Boomers don't usually respond well to authority figures: They may come across with an "I already know all that" attitude.

They respond best to educators who treat them as equals and share personal examples of their own knowledge and skills. Beware of overfamiliarity, however. Do not alienate veterans while accommodating boomers by relating personal anecdotes.

Teaching considerations

Baby boomers are motivated to learn if newly acquired knowledge and skills will help them excel on the job and gain recognition. Consider these tips when planning education for baby boomers:

- Correlate the educational activities with improved job performance.

- Incorporate interactive educational activities such as icebreakers and discussions. Boomers are team-oriented and enjoy team learning activities.

- Avoid role-playing activities; most boomers do not like them.

- Allow time for private practice. Like most adult learners, boomers don't like to display lack of knowledge or skill in public.

- Use learning activities that provide personal challenges and allow baby boomers to use of life experiences.

- Make information easily and readily accessible. Remember, this was the first generation to use the Internet.

Generation X

Generation Xers, born between 1961 and 1980, have also been called "the latchkey generation." Defining events of their lives included Watergate, President Nixon's resignation, the growing trend of single-parent families, and the increasing use of computers as part of their everyday lives.

In contrast to the baby boomers who thrive on and often "live to work" the Xers work to live and value a reasonable balance between work and personal time. Xers value flexibility, dislike close supervision, and prefer self-directed learning. Xers are comfortable with change and see it as the norm rather than the exception. Xers have seen their parents' experience with downsizing and are accustomed to changes in their parents' financial status and changes in family structures. Having seen first-hand the effects of downsizing, Xers are not loyal to a particular organization; they are loyal to themselves. Their attitude can be described as, "It's only a job."

Teaching considerations

Be aware that there are distinct differences—even conflicts—between the ways boomers and Xers view the world, adopt a work ethic, and value education and training. These differences can make it a challenge for them to work together. Generation Xers do not need or even want classroom interaction or team activities. They prefer self-directed learning at a time and place convenient for them. They dislike having to be at a specific place at a specific time to participate in learning activities. Xers are born distance learners. Here are more tips for involving Xers in teaching/learning activities:

- Make learning activities fun—Xers value fun as part of any work or learning activity.

- Include hands-on learning activities and activities in which learners learn by doing. Xers love role-playing scenarios, and they are not worried about making mistakes in front of others as they learn.

- Allow plenty of time for discussion, especially if you are teaching in a classroom setting. Xers are enthusiastic learners and ask lots of questions. If distance learning is the teaching method, clearly identify how their questions will be answered (e.g., e-mail, face-to-face meetings, etc.).

- Be clear about your availability to answer questions. Xers want educators to be available to answer questions and facilitate learning, but they do not want to feel pressured or crowded. They need their freedom.

- Earn their respect early by demonstrating your expertise and enthusiasm to help them learn. Xers do not automatically respect authority figures, including educators. You need to earn it.

- Include a lot of visual stimulation (e.g., graphics, tables, pictures, etc.). Xers don't read as much as the boomers, they prefer these visual methods over printed narratives.

Generation Net

Generation Net, born between 1981 and 1997, is also referred to as the Echo-Boom Generation. An estimated 80 million Netters will displace the 77 million baby boomers and the 44 million Xers and redefine the workplace.

This generation has grown up in the technological age. The Internet is as taken for granted for them as the television was for boomers. Generation Net grew up with computers, CD players, and VCRs. They are comfortable with the tools associated with distance learning.

Netters value diversity. They are highly motivated and understand that knowledge and skills will increase their ability to find good jobs. Netters are accustomed to sharing the workload from a young age, as they generally held part-time jobs during high school and college.

Netters are globally oriented thanks to the Internet and other technological advances. They know and understand that there is no such thing as geographic isolation or protection, as illustrated to them by 9/11. Their concept of family is different from that of veterans and boomers—single parenthood, same-sex partnerships, and grandparents as primary parent figures are only some of the ways Netters define their families.

Netters have even less company loyalty than the Xers. They have seen downsizing become almost a norm and have witnessed a constant stream of mergers, takeovers, closings, and acquisitions. Company loyalty is not a factor in their career paths. They anticipate numerous job changes as they pursue their careers. The focus of their work life is not on where they work but on what they do. Netters respect those who demonstrate expertise and knowledge, but they do not necessarily equate these characteristics with age, rank, or tenure.

Teaching considerations

Netters thrive best in work environments that offer them a direct say in how the organization functions and that encourage their input. They want to perform their jobs to the best of their abilities. When planning teaching activities for Netters, think about the following characteristics associated with this generation. Netters

- enjoy the opportunity to interact with their colleagues during training

- have strong work ethics

- look for structure as well as fun in the workplace and during education activities

- enjoy entertaining, varied education activities

- are comfortable with the technology of distance learning but prefer interactive opportunities

- benefit most from mentor programs

- are interested in earning a good living and value education that will increase their ability to earn money

- enjoy creative teaching techniques including the incorporation of music and games

- are readers and value the time they spend reading

Because you'll be dealing with all four generations, plan varied activities that meet at least some of the needs of each generation. Explain why certain techniques are being used to help learners accept the necessity of being involved in activities that do not meet their personal preferences (e.g., role-play for boomers or a strict time table for Xers).

Your CD-ROM contains a chart (Multigenerational teaching techniques organizer, Figure 8.1) that you can customize and to ensure you are implementing teaching methodologies that address every generation in your audience. The chart summarizes the major characteristics of each generation discussed in this chapter. You can use the "Teaching techniques" column to plan specific learning activities that meet the needs of each generation of learners.

References

Alch, M. L. (2000). "Get ready for the Net Generation." *Training,* 37(2), pp. 32–33.

News Digest. (2001). "Baby boomers." *Training* (Electronic version), Retrieved August 24, 2002, at *www.trainingmag.com.*

News Digest. (2001). "Generation Xers." *Training* (Electronic version), 38(1), Retrieved August 24, 2002, at *www.trainingmag.com.*

Zemke, R., Raines, C., and Filipczak, B. (1999). "Generation gaps in the classroom." *Training,* 36(11), pp. 48–54.

Chapter 9

Designing diversity education for a multicultural audience

Staff-development specialists teach learners who represent a variety of cultures. Cultural diversity is a valued component of our society. Educators must consider what effects culture has on learning.

How do you logically incorporate cultural diversity in program planning? The following suggestions can help you develop an organized plan for providing educational products and services to multicultural audiences.

English as a second language

It may be to your organization's advantage to offer an "English as A Second Language" course for employees. Employees whose native language is not English are at a disadvantage when communicating with their English-speaking colleagues and patients. It is impossible to understand diverse cultures if staff members and patients cannot talk to one another. If there is a predominant cultural population of patients and staff within your organization (e.g., Hispanic or Asian), consider offering a course in that population's native language for your English-speaking staff. Many colleges, universities, and high schools offer this type of course. You may be able to negotiate having a course brought on-site at your organization on a regularly. A good place to start negotiations is with any colleges or universities that have student affiliations with your organization.

Justify the expense of this type of education using quality-improvement data from patient-satisfaction surveys, evaluations from educational programs, adverse-occurrence reports related to communication/cultural differences, performance-evaluation data, and orientation feedback from new employees.

Include American culture in diversity education

Although Americans represent a variety of ethnic and racial backgrounds, there are cultural distinctions that are truly American. For example, most Americans value eye contact as an indicator of attention and concentration. Asian and Middle Eastern cultures avoid eye contact and may consider it insulting or an indication of sexual promiscuity, so a nurse who has just arrived from Jordan needs to understand the significance of eye contact to Americans.

Americans also have a reputation of being loud and boisterous. A nurse-colleague related the following experience as she dined in a restaurant with her French husband.

"We were in a small restaurant in a Paris suburb and I overheard the people at the next table speaking English and talking about the upcoming Super Bowl game. I immediately introduced myself as a fellow American and soon we were having an animated conversation about football and where we lived in the United States. After they left the restaurant I noticed that my husband looked rather uncomfortable and embarrassed. I also noticed that other French diners were looking at me. My husband explained that in France, people would never have conversations with strangers simply because they were from the same country. It just isn't done."

When planning diversity education, include American characteristics as well as characteristics of other countries.

Include cultural-diversity training in orientation

It is not easy to add more content to an orientation program. However, use what you know about learning styles and generational differences to include cultural-diversity education in orientation. Role-play, discussion, and distance-learning techniques can all be used to provide basic information. Allow time for face-to-face discussion as well. Include information about how cultural differences manifest themselves in patients, visitors, and colleagues.

How do you determine which cultures to include? Start with those that are most frequently part of your patient and employee populations. Always include predominant facets of American culture, too.

Include cultural diversity as part of your competency training

Cultural diversity should be included as part of your competency training. Because staff need to demonstrate ongoing competency, this will allow you to add aspects of additional cultures as needed. How can staff demonstrate competency? Written tests, role-play, and on-the-job behaviors can demonstrate competency. Incorporate competency assessment techniques that have proved valid within your organization.

What topics should you include as part of diversity education?

It is not possible to include all aspects of multiple cultures. If cultural diversity is part of your competency program, regularly add aspects of various cultures.

Following are aspects to include in your initial training.

- How do members of this culture communicate? What significance do body language, gestures, tone of voice, and eye contact have? Which family members take the lead in communicating with people outside of their culture?

- What specific family/gender issues exist? What is the woman's role? How are major decisions made?

- What role does religion play?

- How is pain expressed?

- What are common health practices? (e.g., alternative medicine, herbal medicine, home remedies, etc.).

- How do families deal with pregnancy and births?

- What is the culture's work ethic? How are specific occupations viewed in terms of respectability, financial need, and appropriateness?

- Are there dietary restrictions associated with this culture?

Many Web sites deal with cultural diversity. Here are two that are helpful: (Type in "cultural diversity in healthcare" in your favorite search engine for more options):

EthnoMed (http://ethnomed.org)—Offers information about cultural beliefs, medical issues, and lifestyles of immigrants to the United States. Emphasis is placed on persons arriving from war-torn parts of the world.

Cultural Diversity in Healthcare presented by Geri-Ann Galanti
(www.ggalanti.com/cultural_profiles)—Profiles a number of cultures including East Indian, European, Russian, Hispanic, Middle Eastern, Asian, African-American, and Anglo-American.

After you have identified the cultures you will include in your diversity education, use the template in Figure 9.1 to customize your plan. Enter a culture and organize the important considerations for that culture under each appropriate heading.

Diversity education planner

FIGURE 9.1

Culture	Characteristics
	Communication • Body language • Gestures • Tone of voice • Eye contact • Spokesperson
	Family/gender • Role of women • Role/importance of children • Head of the family • Family structure • Decision-making process • Sexuality issues (e.g., must the caregiver be the same sex as the patient?)
	Pain • How is it expressed? • How is it viewed? (e.g., devine will, punishment, etc.) • Accepted measures to relieve pain
	Health practices • Pregnancy and births • Cause of illness • Alternative medicine • Home remedies • End of life issues (e.g., organ donation) • Treatments and their appropriateness (e.g., blood transfusions, amputations, etc.) • Suffering
	Diet/nutrition • Restrictions • Preparation • Religious associations

Diversity education planner (cont.)	

FIGURE 9.1

Culture	Characteristics
	Religion • Role in daily life • Specific practices • Clergy representation • Influence on perceptions of illness and injury
	Work ethic • Gender issues • Financial needs • Respectability of specific occupations

References

Galanti, G. A. (2003). *Cultural diversity in Healthcare*. Retrieved April 30, 2004, from *www.ggalanti.com/cultural_profiles*.

Narayan, M. C. (2003). "Cultural assessment and care planning." *Home Healthcare Nurse* (Electronic version), 21(9), pp. 611–618. Retrieved April 27, 2004, from *www.nursingcenter.com*.

UNIT 3

Teaching strategies for adults

Chapter 10

Motivation challenges: Managing resistant learners

One of the basic principles of adult learning is that adults are self-directed learners. But what happens when adults direct themselves not to learn?

All staff-development specialists face the challenge of motivating learners who don't want to participate in a given learning activity. These resistant learners are restless, sometimes rebellious, and often sullen. Their verbal muttering and body language clearly let you know that they do not want to participate, whether the setting be in a classroom, on-the-job, or in a distance-learning environment. Their attitudes affect other learners, making it difficult to establish and maintain a positive learning environment. They may even encourage open rebellion among participants. How can you deal with this problem and maintain a positive attitude?

Resistant learners

There are a few things that you must recognize and accept. The problem of resistant learners is never going to vanish: As long as you are in the education business, you will face learners who seem to make it their vocation to hamper learning activities. This is one of the ongoing challenges that all staff-development specialists face regularly.

Next, don't blame yourself for someone's lack of motivation. True, there are poorly designed and implemented learning activities. However, in most cases, you are not responsible for a colleague's willingness to learn. Evaluate the effectiveness of your programs and make improvements as indicated by their success or lack thereof. But don't assume the responsibility for your colleagues' behaviors and beliefs—and don't let anyone else make you responsible for them either. This goes back to the discussion about values in Unit I. One of your organization's values should be that employees are responsible for their own learning. Your responsibility is to enhance organizational effectiveness and job performance by providing effective, well-designed and well-implemented learning activities, and striving to continually improve the way you deliver education products and services.

> ### TIP
>
> *A learner's resistance may have nothing to do with you or with the education being offered. He or she may be experiencing personal or health problems for example. Perhaps there was a fight with a spouse before coming to work or an on-the-job conflict with a colleague or supervisor? You or your education program may simply be the target of misplaced anger.*

Finally, you will not improve motivation by ignoring or accepting the resistant learners' attitudes and behaviors. This will only make the disruption of the educational activity worse, interfere with willing participants' abilities to learn, and hamper your ability to effectively carry out education. You may need to make some unpopular decisions and take difficult actions to deal with these challenges. This chapter offers steps to deal with the resistant learner. They are not always easy, nor are they 100% effective, but they should help diffuse the negative atmosphere created by resistant learners.

Success factors

Use what you know about adult learning, learning styles, and differences among generations and cultures to assess the quality of the programs you develop. Armed with this knowledge, consider the following success factors in motivating resistant learners.

Is it clearly understood why education is important or mandated?

You may assume that everyone knows why education (e.g., new procedures or customer service training) is necessary. But not everyone has access to the same information, no matter how effectively you believe you and other managers communicate. Part-time employees, employees who spend a lot of time on the road (e.g., visiting nurses, liaison nurses, etc.), and employees who work evenings, weekends, and holidays do not receive the plethora of information conveyed to those who work day shifts. And no matter how hard a busy organization tries to communicate with its staff members, the communication is not always effectively transmitted or accurately received.

Therefore, it is up to you and your staff-development colleagues to clarify the importance of, as well as the rationale for, educational activities. You can do this verbally in classroom settings, in writing, or via audio means for distance-learning activities. Reiterate such explanations in your objectives.

Is the learning activity really necessary?

You have probably been asked to develop an education program to solve a problem that is not the result of insufficient knowledge. For example, suppose several physical-rehabilitation nursing units are having difficulty administering medications on time. Adverse occurrence reports indicate that the cause of these events is a system problem, not a knowledge problem. Medications are scheduled to be administered when many of the patients are away from the units receiving physical therapy and other treatment modalities. It is not possible to change therapy schedules, but it is possible to change routine administration times. Working with the pharmacy, these units were able to change the routine times put in place by the rest of the hospital. For example, once a day means 9 a.m. on most units, but is 8 a.m. on the rehabilitation units.

Suppose management wanted you to conduct a program about correct medication administration to solve this problem. The nurses would certainly have been resistant, and you would be frustrated trying to plan a program that was not needed. Before rushing to develop a program, investigate the issues surrounding the problem. By doing so, you may be able to avoid wasting your time and the time of potential learners.

> **TIP**
>
> *You may need to convince management that education is not an appropriate quick fix for certain problems. Enlist the help of quality-management staff and the managers of the areas affected by these problems. Be able to justify your decision not to provide educational activities with objective data.*

Have you identified your audience?

If you work for a large organization, it is not possible to personally know all of your learners. But there are steps you can take to get to know your audience and their learning styles:

- When you have the opportunity to observe learners (e.g., during a learning activity, on-the-job, or in the cafeteria), do your best to establish a friendly rapport. Learners are more likely to be honest and cooperative if they feel they know you.

- Pay particular attention to the general learning style and the generation of your learners. Use what you know about their characteristics to plan programs.

- Notify your learners as far in advance as possible about education offerings. There will always be the need for just-in-time training, but the needs of adult learners must be considered. They deserve advance notification to arrange schedules, plan for child care if program attendance requires extra hours at work, and do any prerequisite/prelearning activity preparation.

- Emphasize how the content of education programs and services can be applied to their areas of practice and how it can improve job performance.

Are your learners afraid of repercussions if knowledge is not acquired?

Most organizations have certain knowledge requirements such as attaining cardiopulmonary resuscitation (CPR) certification or advanced cardiac life support (ACLS) certification for critical-care personnel. If certification is not attained, employees will lose their jobs or be demoted. Fear of adverse consequences can make people feel and behave negatively about learning activities. Although you cannot alter the consequences, you can provide a supportive environment, ensure that the activity is well-designed and appropriately implemented, and work with management to provide tutoring as appropriate.

Is the educational content offered in manageable increments?

Too much information relayed at too rapid a pace does not allow learners time to absorb information. A complex education program, such as ACLS or spinal-cord injury rehabilitation should be broken into increments, and a variety of teaching techniques should be used. Realistically, however, there is not a great deal of free time in any healthcare organization. As noted in Chapter 3, accelerated learning is growing in importance. Later in this chapter, we'll discuss specific suggestions for accelerated-learning techniques.

Does the staff-development specialist have credibility? Is the content presented accurately?

Learners resist (and may resent) having content presented by an unqualified educator. Examples of this problem include a critical-care course presented by someone who has no critical-care experience, or a computer-based learning program relating to the pathophysiology of spinal cord injury that contains errors or is outdated. Adults expect to gain accurate knowledge and skills during their learning activities. Information that is inaccurate or presented by someone who is not qualified will generally be interpreted by learners as offensive and a waste of their time.

Will learners have the opportunity to apply the new knowledge and skills acquired as a result of a learning activity?

Have you ever been told to develop and implement extensive mandatory education programs for large numbers of staff, only to find that these learners never had the chance to apply the newly acquired skills and knowledge? Perhaps the triggers for these programs were accrediting-agency recommendations or proposals for the delivery of new services or products to a given patient population. Whatever the reason, learners resent not being able to apply what they've learned. One of the basics of adult education is that the learning activity must have relevance to the learners' lives. What can you do under these circumstances? First, find out why learners are unable to put new knowledge and skills to use. If it is resistance from certain managers, you may be able to talk to them and offer to help with the implementation.

If resistance comes from the administrative level of the organization, you can still find out (tactfully) the reason. If you truly believe that implementation is necessary for performance improvement and better patient outcomes, enlist the help of departmental managers, organizational development, and/or quality-improvement staff. Justify your position by pointing out (backed by objective data) why knowledge implementation will enhance organizational effectiveness.

Unfortunately, sometimes a pattern develops when programs are mandated as an attempt to find a quick fix for a noneducation problem. Again, gather objective data to support your claim that certain issues are not the result of lack of knowledge or skills. Also point out that employee dissatisfaction is the result of unnecessary education/situations that prohibit the implementation of new knowledge and skills.

Do you use a variety of teaching techniques?

Classroom presentations must contain more than lecture and discussion. Make sure handouts and visual aids are colorful and appealing. Implement at least one technique for each leaning style. Pay attention to the audio and visual content of distance-learning methodologies.

Do you have an upbeat, positive attitude about education?

If you are bored or negative, your learners will soon be bored and negative, too. You set the tone by your body language, enthusiasm, and ability to encourage learning. This is easier to do face-to-face than in distance learning. However, you can make sure that distance learning activities are well-designed and visually and aurally pleasing.

Do learners feel comfortable in the learning environment?

The environment must be supportive and nonthreatening, regardless of the teaching method. Include questions on the performance evaluation about the emotional comfort of the learning environment. Adults who feel belittled or embarrassed will not be enthusiastic learners.

Dealing with overt hostility

The preceding discussion offers good suggestions, but what do you do when someone becomes downright hostile? Here are two scenarios that offer possible ways to deal with a hostile leaner.

Case study 1: The disruptive learner

You are hired as the manager of staff development for a 500-bed community hospital. One of your first actions is to ensure attendance and participation at mandatory education classes, particularly those that deal with workplace safety. The chief executive officer's (CEO) administrative assistant, Jennifer, has never attended these mandatory training sessions. However, based on recommendations from accrediting organizations, all employees are required to participate in these classes.

Jennifer is angry and resistant. Some components of the program were offered in a classroom setting, and Jennifer arrives about five minutes before the first class begins. She sits in the back of the room and immediately begins to complain loudly about having to attend this program. Some of her complaints include, "I don't see why I have to attend this ridiculous program. I work for the CEO and have better things to do." and "I never had to go to programs before, why should I start now?"

You use a variety of teaching techniques, including fun activities. However, with Jennifer in the room, the atmosphere becomes hostile. You try to be upbeat and positive, clarifying why these programs are important to both employees and customers. You encourage class input and make sure staff expertise and life experiences are acknowledged. However, Jennifer keeps muttering about being bored or that the class activities are ridiculous. Most of the other participants are disgusted by her behavior, but a few of them begin making negative comments, too. What else can you do?

This type of scenario is frustrating and, sadly, not uncommon. However, you cannot allow one person to destroy the learning experience for everyone else. An organization that values education will support you in these situations. Consider arranging a small group activity for the other learners and ask to speak to Jennifer privately. You don't want the conversation to embarrass her—or you. Tell her that it is obvious she doesn't want to participate and is upset, and ask her whether there is anything you could do to help.

If her response is, "Yes, get me out of here," tell her the choice is hers to make. She could stop disrupting the class and show some consideration for her colleagues or return to her work. Always give a choice. It's up to the learner to take responsibility for his or her actions.

What if Jennifer chooses to leave? As she goes, she adds, "Just wait until I tell my boss about you!" The next day you are summoned to the CEO's office. Explain to him or her, as objectively as possible, what had happened, and state that it was Jennifer's choice to leave rather than to stop disrupting the class.

Case study 2: The violent learner

A staff nurse arrives at your office for some tutoring in rhythm-strip interpretation. Mark has 10 years' experience as a medical-surgical nurse, but he is new to cardiac care. His new job depends on his ability to accurately interpret and identify treatment modalities for cardiac dysrhythmias. Mark needs help, but with extra work he will acquire the necessary knowledge and skills.

Mark is obviously angry when he arrives for the appointment. He refuses to sit down and says, "I've been a nurse for 10 years and never had any trouble before. It's the way this stupid course is being taught. You don't know what you're doing." He begins pacing, and you notice his hands are clenched in fists.

In a calm, deliberate tone, ask Mark to sit down and explain to him that you want to make this experience less frustrating for him and to help him gain the necessary cardiac-care skills. He responds by reaching across your desk, grabbing both your arms, and shouting, "I don't need your help." What do you do?

Here are suggestions for dealing with angry or violent learners:

- **Encourage them to sit down.** You should sit down as well. This puts you on equal eye level and helps diffuse anger.

- **Use a calm, measured tone.** Do not raise your voice or let your body language indicate anger or fear.

- **Do not take their anger personally.** Their anger may be with a spouse, another colleague, or a supervisor. They may be feeling ill. You just happen to be the target of displaced anger. That doesn't make it any less frightening, but it does make it easier to maintain your self-control.

- **Actively listen to them.** Maintain eye contact. Nod your head to indicate understanding. Tell them that you are there to help them, but do not allow them to shout or threaten you. Tell them that you will listen to any concerns and will try to help as long as they treat you with respect.

- **Never allow them to stand or sit between you and the exit.** Always make sure you have a way to get out of an office or classroom. If the anger escalates and you feel you are in danger, ask the angry learner to leave your office, classroom, etc. If he or she does not comply with your request, leave the area at once.

- **Know how to get help quickly.** Don't be afraid to call out for help if you are in danger. Know how to summon security personnel. All organizations should have an emergency number to summon help. Make sure you know what to do in the event of this kind of emergency. If you anticipate that a meeting has the potential for violence, ask another colleague to be present. The presence of another person may be all that is needed to diffuse anger.

- **Report the incident.** Never allow violence—threatened or actual—to go unreported. Follow your organization's policies and procedures for reporting these incidents.

Although you cannot make someone learn or be motivated to learn, you can facilitate learning to the best of your ability. By relying on the principles of adult learning and your knowledge of the various learning styles and generational/cultural differences, you can have a significant affect on the enthusiasm of the learners within your organization.

References

Dickerson, P. S. (2003). "Ten tips to help learning." *Journal for Nurses in Staff Development,* September/October 2003, pp. 244–250.

Hequet, M. (2004). "Training no one wants." *Training,* 41(1), pp. 22–28.

Mulvihill, C. (2002). "Dealing with the difficult patient." (Electronic version) Retrieved August 6, 2002, from *www.pitt.edu.*

Snell, N. (1998). "Stand up—Defusing the hostile trainee" (Electronic version). Retrieved August 6, 2002, from *www.trainingmag.com.*

Chapter 11

Resourceful teaching strategies

This chapter concentrates on resourceful teaching strategies appropriate for today's healthcare environment. Once referred to as "creative training techniques," the term "resourceful strategies" better fits the challenges currently facing staff-development specialists.

Historically, creative teaching focused on classroom techniques. Although classroom creativity is still important, on-the-job training and distance learning have assumed equal importance in the staff-development arena. You not only need to be creative, but resourceful as well.

> ## TIP
>
> *Copyright laws regarding the use of printed materials, audiovisuals, music, etc. govern your use of these resources as education tools. Classroom use and the use of material in distance education are considered separate and different by United States Copyright law. Access the U.S. Copyright Office Web site to print guidelines regarding these laws at www.copyright.gov/circs/circ1.html.*

Accelerated learning

Accelerated learning is the process of acquiring knowledge and skills at a rapid rate. Successful accelerated learning depends on a reduced-stress, supportive environment accompanied by the use of resourceful teaching strategies that include visual aids, graphics, music, imagery, and active learner participation. Providing tips to enhance memory is also integral to the accelerated-learning process.

Advances in medical technology and disease recognition and treatment happen almost daily and thus require ongoing continuing education. Healthcare professionals must absorb large amounts of information quickly. Try these techniques to facilitate accelerated learning:

- Use techniques appropriate for all three learning styles. Provide visual triggers such as flash cards, auditory triggers such as reciting information aloud, and kinesthetic triggers such as practicing psychomotor skills.

- Incorporate the unusual. Learners remember unusual triggers best. Learning activities should be accompanied by music, role-play, games, etc.

- Include frequent breaks during learning activities. This is necessary whether the activity is in the classroom or part of distance learning. For example, during a computer-based program, alternate presentation of information with an interactive session.

- Use a variety of music styles to set the mood. Different types of music promote different types of learning moods. For example, slow pieces such as baroque and chamber music promote tranquility and a relaxed mood. Jazz can stimulate and pep up the mood. Marches and music with percussion instruments can create a high-energy mood as well. Be careful about what music you use as part of your learning activities. If you use music without permission, you may be violating copyright law and will have to pay royalties. The following are sources for royalty-free music. When you call for catalogues, be sure to ask about the policy for using music as part of your education programs:
  – LifeSounds 888/687-4251

       – The Mozart Effect Resource Center 800/721-2177

       – Superlearning 640/731-4569

- Create course themes. Themes must be carefully chosen and should create a relaxed and fun atmosphere, tie course content together, trigger enthusiasm and energy, and stimulate creativity. Consider themes such as solving a mystery, a day at the beach, a scavenger hunt, or a television show.

Resourcefulness in the classroom

The classroom setting is usually popular with adult learners. It allows for interaction, discussion, demonstration, teamwork, role-play, and other activities that stimulate learning. Let's review ideas for enhancing the learning environment in the classroom.

Room setup

How are your classrooms arranged? Do you have the flexibility to physically alter the setting? If you do, think about doing the following:

- Avoid arranging an aisle in the center of your learners seats. The center is really the best place to sit for viewing the educator and any audiovisuals. Place aisles to either side of your audience whenever possible.

- Traditional classroom settings consist of rows of desks or tables facing the front of the room. The educator faces them from behind a podium or desk or stands in front of them. This is a formal structure and can be intimidating for adults. Consider options such as U-shaped groupings of tables or desks, square or rectangle arrangements, or a series of round tables. Round tables are particularly conducive to small group activities.

- Avoid standing behind a desk or podium. This keeps you at a psychological distance from the learners.

- When choosing a room, be aware of the noise distraction from other classrooms, heating and air-conditioning systems, and noise outside the building (e.g., from construction). Change location if needed. If that is not possible, make sure speakers and audio equipment can be heard above the level of the noise. Use a portable microphone to help you in these situations.

- Lights with dimmers are an asset. They allow minimal light for note-taking when using various audiovisuals (AVs) without producing glare.

- If you have input into the selection of wall, floor, and chair covering, remember that floral, striped, or vivid colors such as red are distracting. Avoid them. Solid shades in soft colors are preferable.

- Before your programs, check out the sound level. Stand in various parts of the room, ask your presenters to speak, and check the audio portion of any equipment.

- Don't use chairs with rigid backs such as stack chairs. The backs of chairs should support the lower back and be sturdy. When possible choose chairs that are easy to move.

- Avoid placing distracting objects such as paintings or sculpture on walls. However, if you are decorating the room as part of a theme (e.g., "A Day at the Beach"), appropriate décor is acceptable as long as it enhances the learning experience.

- If you can, arrange electrical outlets to be placed every 6 ft along the walls. Ideally, telephone jacks should be located next to the outlets for conference calls, audioconferences, and computer hookups. Think about cable television outlets when making future design plans. The popularity of cable modems is rapidly increasing.

TIP

Always have electric adaptors available. You may have trouble with two-or three-pronged plugs that don't match outlets.

AV aids

Following are tips when dealing with AV aids, including those used in distance learning. A chart that organizes these tips appears on the CD-ROM, which you can customize to create a quick reference tool.

TIP

Remember to double check all of your AV equipment to make sure it's working properly at least 30 minutes before your program is scheduled to begin. For distance learning, set up a regular maintenance schedule for computers, software, DVD players, etc.

Overhead transparencies/slides/Powerpoint presentations

- Limit each visual to one idea. Avoid elaborate diagrams and graphics that are difficult to see.

- Go to the back of the classroom and make sure you can clearly see/read the information.

- Use at least an 18-point type.

- Avoid ornate fonts. Arial is generally easy to read in most mediums, including computer-based learning.

- Vary the size of the type to emphasize the importance of various statements.

- State concepts in as few words as possible. Too many words reduce the size of the type you are able to use. (e.g., "In the event of an emergency dial 911" is not as effective as "Dial 911 in emergencies").

- Use active verbs and short phrases.

- Use bullet lists to present essential concepts. People like what they can quickly understand and retain.

- Do not use more than three colors.

- Do not use more than two different type styles.

- Do not use vertical lettering. It's hard to read.

- Use pictures, cartoons, etc. when appropriate. Learners usually enjoy this intervention and can easily remember information presented in this format. *(Note: Be careful not to infringe on copyright laws.)*

- Be careful about choosing color combinations. A dark blue background with white lettering can be easy to read, but a yellow background with white lettering might not be.

- Stick to five to six words per line and no more than five lines per slide.

- Powerpoint allows you to add sounds and moving visuals to your presentations. Add audio components only when they enhance learning. Do the same with visuals. It is easy to get carried away and have each line of text fly onto the slide accompanied by sound effects. But too much of this can be distracting.

- Use a remote control so you can face the audience.

Audiotapes, videos, and DVDs

- These tools should be professionally manufactured whenever possible. Home-made audios and videos are rarely appropriate for professional education presentations.

- Review all such tools for accuracy prior to use.

- Make sure that necessary equipment (i.e., tape recorders, VCRs, DVD players) is in good working order. If learners are going to use them as a self-learning activity and you will not be present, make sure extra batteries are available for tape recorders, that videos are readily available, and so on.

Handouts

(Note: Many of the preceding recommendations for slides and transparencies are also applicable for written handouts.)

- Use a 14-point type whenever possible.

- Use color and graphics to liven up handouts and offer different ways of learning.

- Include Web site addresses in your list of references. Most learners will welcome good Internet resources.

Learning activities

Although some lecture is usually necessary, include learning methods that allow learners to actively participate. Here are suggestions for involving your learners in the learning process.

Group activities

Group activities are welcomed by boomers, Netters, and Xers if they believe they will have fun while participating. Veterans may be more hesitant. Prior to initiating group activities, make sure the learners have the necessary knowledge and skills to effectively participate. Remember, you don't want them to be embarrassed in front of their colleagues.

Group leaders help stimulate the learners during these activities. You and other staff-development specialists can function as group leaders, or the learners themselves can select a leader from each group. Group leaders need to be sure that all members have a chance to participate and that no one learner dominates the group. Also do the following:

- Make sure that the group activity will enhance learning. Don't include group activities unless they serve a purpose.

- Sit participants at round tables.

- Give clear directions, both verbally and in writing. Explain the purpose of the group activity, objectives, and what each group is expected to accomplish and present to the entire class at the end of the activity.

- Remember that music can help set the tone of the activity. For example, classical music can aid meditative activities and rousing marches can stimulate. Again, make sure to choose royalty-free music.

- Avoid giving the impression that you or the group leaders are judging or eavesdropping on the groups.

- Set the tone by being upbeat and enthusiastic.

Possible group activities

Debate

Two groups, under the tactful moderation of the staff-development specialist, present two sides of an issue. An interesting tactic is to ask members to defend the opposite side of the debate issue. For instance, suppose that the issue for debate is an ethical one. The situation is that of an elderly patient who is terminally ill, but hasn't been told. Her family is adamant that she not be told. The patient keeps asking the doctors and nurses to tell her what is wrong. Some of your learners agree with the family and some believe that the patient has the right to know. Ask the learners who agree with the family to defend the patient's right to know. Ask the learners who believe that the patient should be told to defend the family's wishes. This twist can help learners understand both sides of the issue and helps to diffuse the potential for uncomfortable disagreements between groups. Although this doesn't always work, it is an interesting option.

Panel

Each group functions as a panel, discussing a particular issue in front of the other groups. A moderator facilitates the presentation and ensuing discussions.

Role playing

Role playing is most effective when acting out an interpersonal skill or human-relations situation. Each role play should be followed by analysis and evaluation of the situation. Remember that boomers may be reluctant to participate in role play.

Demonstrations and return demonstrations

These are especially effective when psychomotor skill acquisition is necessary.

Resourceful teaching is an essential ability of the staff-development specialist. One of the most interesting challenges to this resourcefulness is how and when to use distance learning. The next chapter focuses on distance learning and how to decide what learning activities are most appropriate for teaching at a distance.

References

Craig, R. L. (Ed.). (1996). *The ASTD training & development handbook. A Guide to human resource development* (4th ed.). New York: McGraw-Hill.

Meier, D. (2000). *The accelerated learning handbook.* New York: McGraw-Hill.

O'Conner Finch, M., Virgil, G. (2001). "Teaching/learning methodologies." In A. E. Avillion (Ed.). *Core curriculum for staff development* (2nd ed.) pp. 231–261.

Pike, R. W. (1994). *Creative training techniques handbook* (2nd ed.). Minneapolis: Lakewood Publications.

Pike, R. W. (2003). *Creative training techniques handbook* (3rd ed.). Minneapolis: Lakewood Publications.

Rose, C., and Nicholl, M. J. (1997). *Accelerated learning for the 21st century.* New York: Dell Publishing

Chapter 12

Distance learning

When asked about learning preferences, many, if not most, learners say they prefer the live, interpersonal, face-to-face classroom setting. They like the interaction among learners and educators, and many admit they enjoy the break in their work routine. However, all healthcare staff-development specialists know that it is becoming increasingly difficult to allow learners to take time away from their work. So, what's the answer?

The answer is finding the right mix of classroom and distance, self-learning strategies. A popular term to describe this right mix is blended learning. Blended learning is the combination of many types of learning activities (e.g., classrooms, on-the-job training, distance learning, skills labs, etc.) to best meet learners' needs. This chapter focuses on distance learning, because the need for education that learners can access at times convenient to their schedules continues to grow. Distance learning encompasses a wide range of techniques that are implemented "at a distance" from a centralized education location. The fastest growing distance-learning strategy is e-learning. In fact, many staff development specialists are now in the process of converting some classroom learning activities to e-learning activities.

Deciding which programs to convert to e-learning

Here are criteria for deciding which of your current programs would be effective e-learning courses:

Programs that require strict consistency of content: Health Insurance Portability and Accountability Act of 1996 training, infection control, and similar mandatory courses are potential e-learning topics.

Programs that must reach large numbers of employees quickly: For example, aspects of orientation and new hospital- or departmentwide policies or procedures.

Learning activities that affect small numbers of employees infrequently: For instance, education needed to work within a specific specialty (e.g., stroke rehabilitation).

Learning activities that change frequently but affect many employees: It seems that new medications affect healthcare practice almost daily. Developing an intrasystem medication update accessed via computer-based learning might save considerable time and money. Access to this type of education would enable large numbers of healthcare workers to stay up to date on the latest medications and their uses. Updates only need to be entered into the program once, thus saving educator time and effort.

Starting a distance-learning initiative

Do your learners have the knowledge and skill to access and participate in e-learning? Perhaps the first e-learning course should be an assessment of learners' computer competency. In fact, computer literacy should be part of your organization's competency program. It will soon be difficult to find a job that does not require at least minimal computer skills.

There are many e-learning companies that specialize in healthcare education. These companies frequently contract with particular healthcare systems to provide e-learning at reduced costs for their clients. Just type in "continuing education for healthcare professionals" in your favorite search engine and you'll be amazed by how many responses you receive. Be sure to use the phrase "continuing education." If you just use "education," you're likely to receive most of your hits from colleges and universities publicizing formal academic programs.

Strategies for blended learning

Research indicates that learners who are enthusiastic about distance learning are highly motivated, self-disciplined, and serious about obtaining education. To facilitate the use of e-learning among all employees, you need to help them redefine their concepts of learning environments.

The picture of a formal classroom setting immediately comes to mind when you ask staff to think about education. Generation Xers and Netters are the most likely generations to quickly adapt to e-learning as a normal education source. Learning environments are without geographic limitations. Your learners may be down the hall, in the next state, or in another country. The new learning environment is one in which learners share a common purpose and communicate through the written word as well as the occasional personal encounter. Holding conference calls via computer enables you to both see and write to your students. In the near future, such virtual classrooms allowing written, visual, and audio interaction will become commonplace.

Distance learning can be used as the only educational medium or in combination with classroom work. Consider using distance education for self-tutorials or for preliminary work in acquiring new knowledge and psychomotor skills. After learners are comfortable with didactic knowledge and pass a written assessment of this knowledge, they could move to a clinical laboratory setting to practice and demonstrate newly acquired psychomotor skills. You may be able to create challenge exams that employees new to the organization or to a specialty can take and thus opt out of certain aspects of classroom orientation. For example, if nurses have extensive cardiac care experience, they can participate in interactive e-learning and demonstrate their proficiency in skills such as arrhythmia recognition and management. This will decrease the need for classroom orientation and enable nurses to complete orientation more quickly.

Never attempt to develop e-learning without the support and assistance of your organization's e-learning experts. These are the people who will prevent you from wasting significant time and money on developing programs that your organization's electronic systems can not sustain.

The next unit offers teaching tips for specific situations such as orientation and inservice training. Using e-learning as a technique to facilitate these programs is encouraged. Make e-learning a valuable component of your education products and services.

References

Johnson, G. (2003). "Brewing the perfect blend." *Training*, 40(12), pp. 30–34.

Johnson, G. (2004). "Conversion anxiety." *Training*, 41(2), pp. 34–40.

Palloff, R. M., & Pratt, K. (1999). *Building learning communities in cyberspace.* San Francisco: Jossey-Bass.

Chapter 13

From novice to expert: A framework for meeting learner needs

In 1984, Patricia Benner, PhD, RN, published the results of a descriptive nursing study that identified five levels of competency in clinical nursing practice. Although based on dialogues with nurses, this framework can be applied to almost anyone who works in healthcare. As you plan your programs, think about learner needs based on their experiences in their chosen professions.

Using Benner's framework for program planning

Brief descriptions of each level of learner identified by Benner are offered as a trigger for your planning. Following the descriptions are suggested teaching tips for that level. All of this information is summarized in a chart on your CD-ROM.

> **TIP**
>
> *Benner's is not the only framework for clinical practice. Explore healthcare literature to find other resources to guide your educational practice. Benner's framework is emphasized here because of its adaptability for the development of useful learning activities.*

Level I: Novice

The novice is a beginner in his or her chosen profession. Novices have no experience as professionals in their work-related environments. They need objective, concrete learning situations. Although they possess the intellectual knowledge of academic training, they need opportunities to apply their knowledge as skills in the actual work-setting. They also need a supportive environment with mentors who are eager to help colleagues enter the healthcare setting.

Teaching considerations

- Offer case studies to allow novice learners to practice translating knowledge into practice.

- Encourage mentorships with more experienced nurses.

- Offer programs that add to their basic knowledge. Didactic programs combined with opportunities to discuss translating knowledge into practice meet their needs.

- Give novice learners opportunities to demonstrate newly acquired psychomotor skills

Level II: Advanced beginner

Advanced beginners are able to demonstrate marginally acceptable performance. They have dealt with enough real-life situations to recognize their most meaningful aspects and intervene appropriately in similar situations. They begin to rely on guidelines formed from their own experience.

Teaching considerations

- Offer these learners activities that give them a chance to use their experiences to acquire new knowledge

- Interactive e-learning, lecture/discussion, case studies, and role-play offer opportunities to improve organizational skills and prioritize work loads

- Advanced beginners benefit from mentoring opportunities

Level III: Competent

Competent clinicians have worked in the same or similar environments for at least two to three years. They view their actions in terms of long-range plans as they organize and prioritize tasks that must be completed.

Teaching considerations

- Give these learners opportunities to develop leadership skills

- They value programs that provide updates and recent advances in their specialties.

- They enjoy interactive learning and more complex case studies than the previous two levels.

- Allow them opportunities to partner with proficient and expert learners (see following descriptions) during learning activities.

Level IV: Proficient

Proficient clinicians look at situations as a whole rather than breaking them down into guidelines or isolated tasks. They are able to anticipate events in given situations based on their past experiences. They can plan ahead with a fair amount of certainty.

Teaching considerations

- These learners benefit from learning activities that present a challenge.

- Provide opportunities to develop instincts and intuition such as interactive case studies presented via e-learning.

- The previous three levels look to proficients for assistance. Proficients need to develop leadership skills, so leadership training is a good idea.

- Proficients should receive formal mentorship training.

Level V: Expert

Experts no longer rely on analytic principles, nor do they need to refer to past experiences to grasp the important elements of a situation. Experts have an instinctive, intuitive grasp of each work-related situation. They are able to quickly focus on the crux of a problem and intervene appropriately without considering a large range of alternative solutions.

Teaching considerations

- Experts need to have quick access to advances in their given specialties

- They need to implement leaderships skills and help others acquire such skills

- Programs on how to facilitate learning among their colleagues are appropriate

- Experts must be able to help assess the quality of their colleagues' work

- Classes on quality management and performance improvement are appropriate

Reference

Benner, P. (1984). *From novice to expert.* Menlo Park, CA: Addison-Wesley Publishing.

UNIT 4

Addressing specific
staff-development challenges

Chapter 14

Compiling
needs-assessment
data

Assessing learners' needs can become an exercise in futility. Have you ever been faced with a mountain of data that is disorganized and makes little or no sense? Needs assessments, although critical, need to be built into existing systems so you don't waste time and effort setting up additional methods of data collection.

Needs assessments are conducted to identify and prioritize learning needs, assess the level of interest in particular education topics, differentiate learning needs from systems or performance problems, and meet accreditation standards. Data come from many sources. You need to be able to track information in a logical, concise manner.

Here are suggestions to ensure an ongoing flow of relevant information concerning learners' educational needs:

1. **Establish a computerized system of documenting and monitoring education needs.** Work with your information-systems department or investigate some of the education tracker software from your vendors.

2. **Determine how you will categorize education topics.** For example, suppose you decide to alphabetize your list of topics, recording not only the topic, but also how many times it was requested and the source of the request (e.g., program evaluations, needs-assessment form, quality-improvement meetings). Where would you file a request such as "Psychological impact of multiple sclerosis (MS) on the patient and family?" Would you record it under mental heath issues, family needs, or MS? Pick the broadest,

easiest to recognize category—in this case MS. If you have more than one person entering needs-assessment data, be sure that everyone involved understands how to categorize and record identified learning needs.

3. **Establish a system for data collection. Identify the sources of your information.** These should include learners, administration, management, performance evaluations, quality-improvement data, and identified trends in healthcare.

4. **Review data on a regularly.** Many organizations plan their education calendars 12 months in advance, allowing for the addition of unexpected programs that are of critical importance. Review data at least quarterly.

Using data from program evaluations

Your goal should be to make data collection as easy as possible. Most education program evaluations include questions about additional learner needs such as, "What education topics would you like to see presented in the future?" This is too vague. You'll get all kinds of responses, including requests that have nothing to do with education (e.g., "We need more employee parking."). When requesting information about learners' education needs on program evaluations, consider rephrasing the question(s) to gain the data you really need. For example, ask staff to identify three

- specific education topics that would improve their ability to do their job

- education programs that they would enjoy attending

- specific education topics that would improve their ability to provide patient care

These questions will help you differentiate between programs designed to improve job performance and those that may simply be topics of interest without job relevance.

> **TIP**
>
> *Don't let data from program evaluations accumulate. Get in the habit of recording education needs identified from program evaluations as soon as you collect them.*

Data from quality-improvement findings

How do you access quality improvement data that are relevant to education planning?

Ideally, you or a staff-development colleague should be a member of the quality-improvement committee. As a member, you will have first-hand knowledge of trends that affect patient outcomes and other organizational services. You will also have the opportunity to teach other members of the committee how to differentiate between learning needs and systems and performance problems. For example, an increase in patient falls on a particular unit does not necessarily indicate a lack of employee knowledge. Work with the quality-improvement committee to analyze the problem. Has there been a change in patient acuity or staffing patterns? When do the majority of falls take place? Are staff members assessing patients' needs inaccurately? By answering these questions, you can determine whether the problem is due to a systems failure, a lack of knowledge or implementation of knowledge, or a combination of both. Once this is determined, you can take appropriate intervention.

Record learning-needs data obtained from this committee under the umbrella of quality improvement. Then compare these data with needs identified by learners and identify similarities and differences. This will also help you to determine whether staff members are aware of quality-improvement issues within the organization.

Data from performance evaluations

Performance evaluations are confidential. You should not have access to evaluations throughout the organization. So how do you obtain necessary data?

An organization that values education will help you establish a system for collecting this data. Performance evaluations are conducted frequently in any organization. A logical way to obtain these data is to establish a regular system of collection. Build it into each department's quality-improvement program. Managers should be required to summarize learner needs obtained from performance evaluations quarterly and give this information to you. They would also alert you to any trends needing immediate attention whenever they are identified. Compare these findings with quality-improvement data and data obtained from learners themselves.

Other sources of data

At this point you have established an ongoing system of data collection from three critical sources: learners, quality-improvement findings, and performance evaluations. But suppose you want more information, such as the learners' years of experience in a given profession or what factors hinder or help them perform their jobs.

Obtaining this information could be part of an annual needs-assessment survey. Only collect data that will be helpful to you. For instance, do you really need to know what unit someone works on? You already have information about trends and needs from performance evaluations and quality-improvement findings that indicate problem locations. If you have a genuine need for this information, fine. But don't ask for it simply because it's always been part of the needs-assessment form.

It's usually a waste of time and effort to distribute these forms via intraorganization mail or even electronically. Most people just don't consider completing an annual needs-assessment form a high priority. Instead, look for events that large numbers of employees attend. For example, does your hospital offer Nurse Week events or hold an employee appreciation day? Consider distributing needs-assessment surveys at major events and offer a simple reward (e.g., pens, discount coupons) for those who complete the survey. Make it easy for yourself. Find an event that already gathers large numbers of employees and incorporate your needs assessment into the process.

A sample needs-assessment form appears in Figure 14.1. There is space to add disciplines, job titles, or more questions if you wish. The questions about factors that help and hinder job performance can be used to trigger education topics, especially if they reflect data obtained from other sources. If you are distributing the survey for learners to complete at their leisure, add a deadline for completion and list where they should bring the completed survey.

Sample needs-assessment form

FIGURE 14.1

Please complete the following education needs-assessment survey. The staff-development department will use this information to plan programs for the coming year. These programs will be designed to improve job performance and patient outcomes. Thank you for your participation!

Date: _____

Name (Optional): _____

Discipline: RN _____ LPN _____ CNA _____ PT _____ OT _____

SLP _____ SW _____ Pharmacist _____

Information systems specialist _____

Organizational development specialist _____

Manager (please indicate discipline) _____

Years of experience in your discipline: _____

1. Identify three education programs that you would attend to help you improve your job performance. _____
   _____
   _____
   _____

2. Identify three things that interfere with your ability to do your job. _____
   _____
   _____
   _____

3. Identify three things that help you to do your job. _____
   _____
   _____
   _____

Sample needs-assessment form (cont.)

FIGURE 14.1

4. Are you comfortable attending education programs that are offered via computer-based learning?   Yes ___   No ___

If not, what would help you to become more comfortable? _____

_____

_____

_____

5. How do you most prefer to obtain education?

Classroom setting————————— Computer-based learning —————————

Video/DVD————————— Audiotapes or audioconferences —————————

Skills lab————————— Self-learning packets—————————

E-mail updates ————————— On-the-job demonstration —————————

Other—————————

_____

_____

_____

6. Please let us know if you have additional comments or suggestions to improve staff-development services. —————————————————————

_____

_____

_____

Chapter 15

Orientation

Most staff-development specialists groan when asked to evaluate and update their orientation programs. One of the few certainties in healthcare staff development is that orientation is in a constant state of revision.

If you have enough staff-development specialists in your department, assign one or two the responsibility for ongoing assessment of orientation. This helps to keep track of the success (or lack of success) of orientation efforts. Answer the following questions as you begin your assessment process:

- Are you responsible for orienting a specific department or do you have responsibility for some aspects of orientation for all new employees?

- What particular aspects of orientation are your responsibility?

- Who provides departmental orientation? Do you have any responsibilities for clinical orientation? If so, do you have clinical educators who perform this duty?

- How often do you hold orientation classes? Is orientation regularly scheduled, or is it done on an as-needed basis?

- How do new employees evaluate the orientation process?

The answers to these questions determine how you design your orientation program. Try to arrange a regular time or times each month for orientation. Because of current staffing shortages, you may be pressured to orient new employees on demand. This can be disastrous. Clinical preceptors/mentors need time to orient colleagues properly, and so do you. Inadequate orientation inevitably leads to early resignation and a significant loss of the organization's time and money.

Arrange orientation classes and self-learning activities in conjunction with other programs as often as possible. For example, if there is a certain skill that all employees must demonstrate annually (e.g., proper use of fire extinguishers) arrange for these monitored demonstrations to take place when new employees are present. This allows both new and current employees to meet a mandatory requirement without the staff-development department having to schedule numerous, unplanned demonstrations.

Preceptors and mentors

If clinical orientation is the responsibility of clinical educators or staff nurse mentors/ preceptors, make sure these individuals have received formal training in mentoring, preceptorships, and adult education. It is highly recommended that those who function as mentors/ preceptors receive financial compensation for these extra responsibilities. The most successful preceptor/mentor programs are part of a clinical ladder that makes attainment of these roles part of a job promotion. Do the following when developing your preceptor/mentor training program:

- Establish a specified amount of clinical experience as a requirement for becoming a preceptor/mentor.

- Select individuals who have demonstrated not only clinical competence, but a genuine desire to help their colleagues excel at their jobs.

- Do not force anyone to become a preceptor/mentor. Candidates for this role must want such responsibilities.

- When designing a curriculum for preceptors/mentors include the following topics:
    - Principles of adult education

- Learning styles

- Generational differences

- How to offer constructive criticism

- How to evaluate clinical performance

- Leadership principles

- Communication skills

Designing a competency-based program

Design your orientation as a competency-based system. Such a system acknowledges and builds on previous knowledge and skills. The orientee should be able to demonstrate knowledge and test out of certain areas of competency. For example, experienced pediatric nurses should not have to sit in a classroom or participate in extensive e-learning on pediatric medication administration. They should have the opportunity to take a challenge test and, upon successful completion of the test, move forward in the orientation.

When possible, establish mechanisms that allow competency demonstration. This decreases hours spent in orientation and allows experienced employees to progress rapidly through the orientation process. Do not reinvent the wheel. Use mechanisms already in place for assessing ongoing employee competency to evaluate orientee competency. Do not develop separate competency programs just for new employees. If you do this you'll waste a lot of time and money developing different learning activities that consist of primarily the same content.

There are limitations to developing and implementing this type of orientation program. The initial development takes time and is costly. There must be an adequate way to document competency. (Use the same competency-documentation forms that have already been established for assessment of current employees). However, after the initial program is in place, advantages far outweigh the limitations:

- The new employees are presented with clear, measurable performance expectations

- Competency demonstration is based on department-specific knowledge and skills

- Orientation time is decreased for experienced professionals

- Competency-based orientation establishes an objective system to document competence

- Preceptors/mentors and managers have a comprehensive foundation for performance evaluation

- The cost of orientation is decreased because new employees are able to test out of areas in which they are competent

- It provides new employees with a consistent orientation program

In summary, orientation should be competency-based. On-the-job preceptors/mentors should receive training in the art of their roles. Use the same competency programs for new and current employees. Finally, when evaluating your orientation program, look for areas where orientation can be combined with already established programs that meet the needs of learners within the organization.

Reference

Gloe, D. (2001). "Implementation of learning activities." In A. E. Avillion (Ed.) *Core curriculum for staff development* (2nd ed.) pp. 261–302. Pensacola, FL: The National Nursing Staff Development Organization (NNSDO).

Chapter 16

Mandatory education

All organizations mandate particular education components for employees. These types of required learning activities are usually conducted on a regular (i.e., annually) schedule. Mandatory programs include but are not limited to those dealing with safety issues, infection control, violence in the workplace, the Health Insurance Portability and Accountability Act of 1996, and so on. As mentioned in the previous chapter, streamline your efforts when possible to meet the needs of more than one group of learners.

If you have selected an interactive computer-based learning package for some of your mandatory training, make sure your learners know how to use these programs and that they have adequate access to computers.

How do you organize attendance at required classes? Many organizations have arranged mandatory monthly learning activities. If you do this, make sure your orientation program coincides with the day(s) that mandatory training is being offered. Arranging a particular day(s) each month allows employees and orientees alike to fulfill mandatory requirements.

Your mandatory classes are probably a blend of classroom, demonstration, and self-learning methods (including e-learning). Set up a classroom and arrange for didactic components and skills demonstrations to be offered at regular intervals throughout the day. (If you work for a large health system you may need to offer these classes around the clock).

Have a number of computers and other self-learning tools (e.g., video, DVD players) available, too. Most employees find it difficult to leave their work areas for an hour at a time on different days to fulfill mandatory training requirements. However, if you arrange day-long events, employees can be scheduled for an education day, fulfill their mandatory education requirements, and know that they will not need to worry about returning to their work areas.

Incorporate competencies into your mandatory training events. This enables objective measurement and documentation of skill or knowledge accomplishment, not just that employees attended particular programs. Whenever possible, use a computerized system to track education attendance.

TIP

Don't forget to ask employees to complete an education needs assessment during mandatory education programs. This is a good opportunity to reach large numbers of employees.

Consider providing opportunities for employees to test out of particular mandatory education classes. For example, experienced clinicians do not necessarily need to sit in a class watching a video and hearing a didactic lecture about cardiopulmonary resuscitation (CPR). Consider giving these employees the opportunity to take a written test and demonstrate CPR without sitting through a lengthy program. (Check with your sponsoring CPR organization, usually the American Heart Association or the Red Cross, to make sure that this option meets their recertification requirements).

Do what you can to make mandatory training less tedious and more enjoyable. Incorporate role-play, case studies, and other group activities when possible. Vary the techniques from year to year. You may need to stay within the same format (e.g., a day-long event, test-out options) but change the way specific content is delivered. If you used a lecture discussion technique for one component of mandatory training this year, switch to a case-study approach next year. Although the content may be similar, the approach can change. This will keep both you and your learners from becoming bored.

Remember that your organization may add or delete certain components of mandatory training based on organizational needs and accrediting standards. Be flexible. Avoid becoming too rigid about fixed time frames for specific components of mandatory education. Remember to ask learners to evaluate mandatory education classes—they may have good suggestions to improve the delivery of this type of education.

Chapter 17

Inservice education

Inservice education generally refers to simple, short-term programming that meets an immediate need. The best example of inservice education is on-the-job training, sometimes referred to as just-in-time training. In other words, it's learning what you need when you need it. Inservice education often involves the need to master a new piece of patient-care equipment quickly, provide quality patient care for a patient with an unusual/unfamiliar illness or injury, or implement a new/updated policy or procedure immediately.

Inservice education is a quick response to changes in your work environment. These types of education needs produce a special challenge for staff development specialists. They are usually unexpected, allowing little time for program preparation and implementation, and require swift demonstration and validation of competency. Successful implementation of inservice education requires the following:

- An educator who is adequately qualified to present information and is ready and willing to teach

- Learners who are ready and willing to learn and eager to help their colleagues learn

- The availability of necessary equipment, documents, etc.

Fulfilling these requirements is not easy. Let's review common examples of inservice training and how to implement them successfully.

New policies or regulations

The immediacy of inservice education is reserved for those policies and regulations that affect patient outcomes; patient, visitor, or employee safety; and accreditation status. If these changes are not complex, their success may require only that employees read and sign documents to verify that they understand and accept the changes.

If this is the case, don't waste your time planning programs that consist of an educator reading a document to a group of learners. Within large organizations, e-learning may be the answer for the majority of employees. Posting the new policy or regulation on the organization's Web site or distributing e-mails may solve the problem. If your organization does not have the capability of employees using an electronic signature to indicate they have read and understood the new guidelines, copies of the guidelines can be e-mailed to department managers. Guidelines accompanied by a signature sheet can be posted in work areas. Employees can sign that sheet after they have read the new policies or regulations. Managers of small departments may choose to present the new information during a staff meeting and ask their employees to sign off then.

Try to ensure consistency regarding how employees indicate their understanding and acceptance. Develop a template that can quickly be customized and distributed to the appropriate work areas. Adapt the following template (Figure 17.1) for the purpose of documenting your inservice education.

FIGURE 17.1

Inservice documentation form (new policies/regulations)

Date: _____

Department/Unit: _____

Distribution of the following new organizational policy(ies)/regulation(s): _____
_____

The attached document(s) indicates a change in or a new way of providing products and services to our patients, families, visitors, and/or employees. After you have read these documents, indicate that you understand and accept these changes or additions by dating and signing below. If you have any questions, please contact your department manager.

It is required that all employees read the attached documents and sign your name by the following date: _____

Date	Signature	Title

New equipment

A scenario that commonly triggers a need for inservice education regarding new equipment involves the transfer or admission of a patient to your organization who is accompanied by a new, unfamiliar piece of equipment necessary for his or her care.

How can you implement training and ensure staff competency? Determine whether anyone within your organization is familiar with this equipment. If the patient is, in fact, a transfer, inquire whether someone from the transferring hospital can accompany the patient to help educate staff. Contact the vendor leasing or selling this equipment. Most vendors have preprinted guidelines for equipment use and are often willing to provide inservices to staff around the clock. Whether you actually do the teaching in this scenario, you must document training and competency. Keep a blank template in your computer to do so.

Inservice documentation form (new equipment)

FIGURE 17.2

Date: _____

Time: _____

Competency: _____

Type of Equipment: _____

Instructor(s): _____

After observing accurate demonstration of _____ the following learners demonstrated competence in the use of _____

_____
Instructor's signature, time, and date

Date	**Time**	**Learner's signature and title**

Develop and keep a template like this in your computer. You can swiftly customize it and distribute it to appropriate departments/units.

Unusual illness or injury

Protocols and treatment modalities will most likely be developed by the clinical patient-care team. However, you will probably need to help your colleagues by researching unfamiliar diseases or injuries. Following are Web sites that will help you when researching this type of challenge:

Centers for Disease Control and Prevention (*www.cdc.gov*)

"The Centers for Disease Control and Prevention (CDC) is recognized as the lead federal agency for protecting the health and safety of people—at home and abroad—providing credible information to enhance health decisions, and promoting health through strong partnerships. CDC serves as the national focus for developing and applying disease prevention and control, environmental health, and health promotion and education activities designed to improve the health of the people of the United States."
Source: CDC Web site.

National Institutes of Health (*www.nih.gov*)

"The National Institutes of Health is the steward of medical and behavioral research for the Nation. It is an Agency under the U.S. Department of Health and Human Services."
Source: NIH Web site.

American Association for Clinical Chemistry (*www.labtestsonline.org*)

This site offers information on a wide variety of lab tests, including rarely ordered tests, and how to interpret findings.

The Food and Drug Administration (*www.fda.gov*)

This site offers a wealth of information about drug trials, approvals, warnings, and cautions.

PubMed (*www.pubmed.gov*)

"PubMed, a service of the National Library of Medicine, includes over 14 million citations for biomedical articles back to the 1950s. These citations are from MEDLINE and additional life-science journals. PubMed includes links to many sites providing full text articles and other related resources."
Source: PubMed Web site.

References

Ellis, K. (2003). "Top training strategies." *Training*, July/August 2003, pp. 31–35.

Puetz, L., and Zuel, S. A. (2001). "Educational planning." In A. E. Avillion (Ed.) *Core curriculum for staff development* (2nd ed.) (pp. 199–229). Pensacola, FL: The National Nursing Staff Development Organization (NNSDO).

Chapter 18

Continuing education

Continuing education is generally defined as learning activities designed to enhance an employee's professional growth and development. These programs, like all learning activities, are ultimately expected to contribute to improvement of job performance and customer satisfaction.

Specific continuing education programs are often identified by learners as educational needs. However, if they are not directly connected to training mandates, competency, or other requirements, it is doubtful that large numbers of learners will be able to leave their work to attend. Every staff-development specialist has spent long hours developing excellent programs only to find few, if any, learners in the classroom. Enthusiastic administrative and management backing is usually the most effective way to improve attendance. Following are tips:

- **Enthusiastic advance publicity.** Select a topic that is bound to trigger interest, such as bioterrorism preparedness or, for oncology nurses, information about the most recently Food and Drug Administration–approved chemotherapeutic agents:

  - Publicize the dates and times of the program

  - Offer the program more than once and during different shifts

- Make use of your organization's computer technology to announce programs

- Make sure these announcements are visually interesting and add audio effects

- Use action verbs to describe what the program is about and how your learners and the organization will benefit from knowledge and skills acquired during this program

- Use bulletin boards located in strategic places such as inside the cafeteria and hospital entrances to promote the program.

- Use bold, colorful words and illustrations to announce your programs

- **Give the learners an added incentive.** You can purchase pens and notepads engraved with virtually anything these days. If your program is about customer service, have notepads printed with the phrase "The Best in Customer Service!" Giveaway incentives are cheap and easy to order. Just type "personalized business gifts" into your favorite online search engine for a multitude of contacts.

- **Encourage word-of-mouth publicity.** Ask learners with whom you have a good rapport to help you promote your programs.

- **Offer credits.** When possible, offer continuing education credits for your programs. This includes programs offered as distance-learning activities.

Consider offering your continuing education programs in several formats. Here are some ideas for delivering continuing education via distance-learning methodologies:

- **Independent, printed study modules.** These could be similar to those offered in professional healthcare journals. If your organization has an organizational newsletter, consider publishing self-study continuing education modules in it.

- **Computer-assisted programs.** These programs can be entertaining and promote interactive learning.

- **Teleconferences.** Popular with healthcare professionals who have limited time and resources to obtain continuing education, this is typically a useful method.

- **Explore partnerships with Web-based healthcare education companies.** As mentioned previously, type "continuing education for healthcare professionals" in your favorite online search engine for an amazing number of results. These companies might be able to take some of the design and coordination burden off your shoulders.

- **Live chats.** These Web-based programs allow participants to interact with learners throughout the world. Organizations that have recently sponsored live chats include the Oncology Nursing Society and CancerresourceRN. Contact professional associations to find out whether they are offering live chats with experts.

Finally, make sure you follow the basic steps of good program planning. Remember to

- assess needs
- identify clear, measurable objectives
- develop a content outline based on these objectives
- develop content using the outline as a road map
- market the program enthusiastically
- implement the program using the most appropriate teaching modalities
- evaluate the effectiveness of the learning activity

Evaluation is the step in the educational process that best demonstrates your effect on organizational effectiveness. The next unit discusses, in detail, evaluation methodologies that help you to demonstrate your worth to your administration, management, and colleagues.

References

Fennimore, L. A. (2002). "Delivering distance learning." In B. E. Puetz and J. W. Aucoin (Eds.) *Conversations in nursing professional development.* pp. 317–328.

Puetz, L., and Zuel, S. A. (2001). "Educational planning." In A. E. Avillion (Ed.) *Core curriculum for staff development* (2nd ed.) pp. 199–229. Pensacola, FL: The National Nursing Staff Development Organization (NNSDO).

UNIT 5

Assessing the effectiveness of education

Chapter 19

An overview of the evaluation process

Once upon a time in staff development, when many education programs were offered, attendance was good, learners enjoyed the activities, and your organization thought you were doing a great job.

Today, you are still expected to offer many programs, promote good attendance, and provide learning activities that participants enjoy, but this does not necessarily mean that you are doing a great job. In the current healthcare environment, you must also demonstrate to the organization that it is worth the time, money, and effort to support education and promote the recruitment and retention of qualified staff-development specialists.

Staff-development specialists are responsible for the effectiveness of their education products and services. You must provide evidence that education improves job performance and enhances patient outcomes. To do this, you need an objective system of data collection and analysis.

The fact that an educator is consistently rated as "highly qualified" and "a good presenter" is important, but it does little to demonstrate the effect education has on organizational effectiveness. On the other hand, if you can document a 40% decrease in patient falls as a result of using knowledge gained from learning activities, you not only helped improve patient safety, but also justified the existence of your education programs.

Arguably, the reduction of patient fall rates does not prove that a specific learning activity was directly responsible for diminished occurrence. However, you can provide objective evidence that indicates a probable link between education and improved outcomes. How do you collect this evidence? You need to determine what types of evaluation strategies to use. Many staff-development specialists refer to these strategies as levels of evaluation, each indicating a progression in complexity. Collecting the data you need requires more than one level of evaluation. The succeeding chapters describe each evaluation strategy and when and how to implement them.

Level one: Reaction/Learner satisfaction. How do the learners feel about the activity? What do the results indicate about the learners' satisfaction with the program?

Level two: Learning. What did the participants learn as a result of the learning activity?

Level three: Behavior. Did the learners' job performance change based on the learning activity?

Level four: Results/Impact. How did behavior changes affect organizational effectiveness?

Level five: Return on investment. How did the learning activity financially affect the organization? What investment in the actual cost of a learning activity was made and what was the return benefit(s) generated by it?

It is not necessary, nor is it efficient, to conduct all five types of evaluation on every program you offer. But you should have a solid understanding of how each can affect the future delivery of your learning activities.

Reference

Abdulhadi, L., and Hull, E. (2001). "Program evaluation and return on investment."
In A. E. Avillion (Ed.) *Core curriculum for staff development.* pp. 343–360. Pensacola, FL: The National Nursing Staff Development Organization (NNSDO).

Chapter 20

Level one: Reaction/Learner satisfaction

At this level, the extent of learner satisfaction with the learning activity is examined. It is sometimes referred to as a "happiness index." Reaction is insufficient as the sole method of evaluation, but it is still extremely important. If learners are bored during the learning activity, feel the material was either too basic or too complex, or believe that the instructor was unqualified or boring, their written and word-of-mouth complaints will quickly destroy the value of a particular education event. The reaction evaluation also provides important information about the physical learning environment, such as whether lighting is adequate, acoustics are good, etc.

Because there are questions specific to both classroom and distance programs, two templates are presented in this chapter. One is for classroom reaction and another is for reaction to distance-learning activities.

The reaction form

A typical reaction form, whether for classroom or distance education, needs to capture the date and time of the event, program title, instructor, and objectives. Fill in the title, instructor's name, and objectives in advance. This ensures consistency and enables the learner to complete the form quickly. By including the objectives, you make it easier for learners to focus on evaluating them, a critical aspect of reaction data. Even though you may verbally explain the objectives and include them on slides or handouts, it is well worth the effort to write the objectives directly on the form.

As mentioned in previous chapters, don't ask for information unless you plan to use it to analyze the success of the learning activity. For example, before you ask learners to identify their profession and work location, decide how you are going to use that information. Are you comparing satisfaction among various disciplines? Do you need to know how many learners participate from specific departments and units? If you don't need the information don't ask for it. You'll have plenty to do just analyzing the data you really need.

Ask how well participants were able to achieve each specific objective. Ask which objectives (if any) were not achieved from the learners' viewpoints. Find out whether the instructor was both interesting and knowledgeable. He or she may be extremely entertaining but ill-prepared or have inadequate knowledge about the education topic. Make sure the educator allowed adequate time and opportunities for discussion and questions. You also need to know whether handouts, audio-visuals (AV), etc. were useful. Also ask learners to evaluate how well they could read handouts and see and hear any AV aids used during the program. The quality of these items greatly affects the learners' satisfaction and ability to achieve objectives. If they can't hear the instructor, or if the video was of poor quality, you need to know. Also, give them an opportunity to rate the comfort of the seating arrangements and classroom temperature.

Here is a template for a simple reaction form (Figure 20.1) for the classroom setting. Feel free to customize the version of this tool that appears on your CD-ROM.

Classroom evaluation form

FIGURE 20.1

Date: _____ Time: _____

Name (Optional): _____

Profession: _____

Department and unit: _____

Program title: _____

Instructor(s): _____

Objectives: 1. _____
          2. _____
          3. _____

Please answer the following questions. (Note: N/A stands for not applicable.)

1. How well did the program content meet the stated objectives?
   ___Excellent ___Very Good ___Good ___Fair ___Poor ___N/A

2. Based on the program content, how well were you able to achieve the objectives?
   a. Objective 1: _____
   ___Excellent ___Very Good ___Good ___Fair ___Poor

   b. Objective 2: _____
   ___Excellent ___Very Good ___Good ___Fair ___Poor

   c. Objective 3: _____
   ___Excellent ___Very Good ___Good ___Fair ___Poor

3. Was the instructor(s) an effective teacher?
   ___Excellent ___Very Good ___Good ___Fair ___Poor ___N/A

4. Was the instructor(s) knowledgeable and well-prepared to teach this program?
   ___Excellent ___Very Good ___Good ___Fair ___Poor ___N/A

Classroom evaluation form (cont.)

FIGURE 20.1

5. Was there enough time for discussion and to ask questions?
    ___Excellent ___Very Good ___Good ___Fair ___Poor ___N/A

6. Did the instructor show respect for the participants?
    ___Excellent ___Very Good ___Good ___Fair ___Poor ___N/A

7. Were the handouts useful?
    ___Excellent ___Very Good ___Good ___Fair ___Poor ___N/A

8. Were you able to read the handouts without difficulty?
    ___Excellent ___Very Good ___Good ___Fair ___Poor ___N/A

9. Were the audio-visuals (AVs) useful?
    ___Excellent ___Very Good ___Good ___Fair ___Poor ___N/A

10. Was the temperature of the classroom comfortable?
    ___Excellent ___Very Good ___Good ___Fair ___Poor ___N/A

11. Were the seating arrangements comfortable?
    ___Excellent ___Very Good ___Good ___Fair ___Poor ___N/A

12. Were you able to see and hear the instructor without difficulty?
    ___Excellent ___Very Good ___Good ___Fair ___Poor ___N/A

13. Were you able to see and hear the AVs used without difficulty?
    ___Excellent ___Very Good ___Good ___Fair ___Poor ___N/A

14. Would you like to make any other comments? _____
_____
_____
_____

15. For future program planning, please identify three specific education topics that would improve
your ability to do your job. _____
_____
_____

Distance-learning activities require much of the same feedback you solicit from classroom activities. Add questions concerning the type of distance-learning technique used and how effective that technique was as a learning activity. Figure 20.2 offers suggestions for the evaluation of reaction to a distance learning experience.

Distance-learning evaluation form

FIGURE 20.2

Date: _____ Time: _____

Name (Optional): _____

Profession: _____

Department and unit: _____

Program title: _____

Teaching method (Please check all that apply):
___Computer-based-learning ___ Video ___Self-learning packet
___Audiotape ___Teleconference

Objectives: 1. _____
            2. _____
            3. _____

Please answer the following questions. (Note: N/A stands for not applicable.)

1. How well did the program content meet the stated objectives?
   ___Excellent ___Very Good ___Good ___Fair ___Poor ___N/A

2. Based on the program content, how well were you able to achieve the objectives?
   a. Objective 1: _____
   ___Excellent ___Very Good ___Good ___Fair ___Poor

Distance-learning evaluation form (cont.)

FIGURE 20.2

b. Objective 2: _____
___Excellent ___Very Good ___Good ___Fair ___Poor

c. Objective 3: _____
___Excellent ___Very Good ___Good ___Fair ___Poor

3. Was the teaching method effective?
___Excellent ___Very Good ___Good ___Fair ___Poor ___N/A

4. How well were you able to use the equipment for this distance-learning experience?
___Excellent ___Very Good ___Good ___Fair ___Poor ___N/A

5. How well did the program explain how to receive help or ask questions if you need to do so?
___Excellent ___Very Good ___Good ___Fair ___Poor ___N/A

6. Were the handouts useful?
___Excellent ___Very Good ___Good ___Fair ___Poor ___N/A

7. Were you able to read the handouts without difficulty?
___Excellent ___Very Good ___Good ___Fair ___Poor ___N/A

8. Was the location of this distance-learning experience comfortable? In other words was it quiet and comfortable?
___Excellent ___Very Good ___Good ___Fair ___Poor ___N/A

9. Did the quality of the graphics, videos, or audiotapes help you learn?
___Excellent ___Very Good ___Good ___Fair ___Poor ___N/A

10. Would you like to make any other comments?
___Excellent ___Very Good ___Good ___Fair ___Poor ___N/A

11. For future program planning, please identify three specific education topics that would improve your ability to do your job. _____

_____

_____

_____

Remember that although it is important, reaction data does not provide evidence that learning took place. This evaluation alone is insufficient. Always try to, at the very least, move to the next level and assess the learners' knowledge gain.

References

Abdulhadi, L., and Hull, E. (2001). "Program evaluation and return on investment." In A. E. Avillion (Ed.) *Core curriculum for staff development.* pp. 343–360. Pensacola, FL: NNSDO.

Avillion, A. E. (1998). *The redesign of nursing staff development.* Pensacola, FL: The National Nursing Staff Development Organization (NNSDO).

Kirkpatrick, D. L. (1998). "Great ideas revisited." In D. L. Kirkpatric (Compiler) *Another look at evaluating training programs.* pp. 3–8). Alexandria, VA: ASTD.

Chapter 21

Level two: Learning

Just because learners loved participating in a particular program doesn't mean they actually learned anything. And, after all, knowledge acquisition is the fundamental purpose of any learning situation. Therefore, how can you efficiently and effectively measure learning?

Your objectives provide the basis for how you evaluate learning. For instance, if the objective is to achieve competence in a psychomotor skill, then safe, accurate demonstration of skill acquisition can measure learning. If the objective is to achieve intellectual, didactic knowledge, then a written test may be the best way to measure learning.

However, to demonstrate that learning actually took place, develop an objective before-and-after approach. For example, if you use a written test as the measurement tool, ask learners to complete the test before and after the learning activity.

TIP

Many interactive computer-based learning programs offer both pre- and posttest options.

The pretest must be done tactfully. Emphasize that the learner's score (or skill demonstration) will be used to demonstrate that learning took place. Assure them that it will not be shared with anyone other than the learner and the educator. No penalties should be involved with the pretest. In fact, if a skill is completely new, record that none of the learners had any experience with this particular skill. This avoids clumsy, embarrassing attempts to perform a psychomotor activity with which the learners are totally unfamiliar.

After you determine the best way to assess knowledge/skills before and after the learning activity, consider the following as part of your evaluation process:

- How clear are your instructions for the completion of pre- and postlearning tests? This is especially important for distance-learning activities when the only way to explain this issue is via the written word or as part of an audio tape.

- Are written materials prepared at the appropriate reading level for the learners?

- Do your written testing materials indicate that employees whose native language is not English are unable to understand what is required of them? (If this is the case, use this information to justify funding to offer English as a second language classes.)

- Are employees whose native language is not English able to follow verbal instructions during psychomotor skill acquisition and demonstrations?

- Do employees understand why it is important to demonstrate learning?

Suppose a large department such as nursing has recently undergone extensive education to institute a complex new treatment regimen that also requires a new psychomotor skill. You have a small staff-development department and are depending on many formal and informal nurse leaders (who have already acquired this skill) to observe accurate demonstration of this new skill. Consider the following points.

- Are these nurse leaders' evaluations consistent? Do they know the exact objectives and how achievement is to be demonstrated?

- Have you made written guidelines available for these nurse leaders? Written guidelines help to ensure consistency of evaluation.

- Have these nurse leaders received any training in dealing with adult learners?

- What happens if someone fails to achieve competence in this new skill? Is extra training available?

TIP

Make sure you have documented that the nurse leaders received training and are competent to perform this skill and evaluate the ability of others to perform it.

Develop a written checklist to accompany guidelines so competency is evaluated on a step-by-step basis. The person doing the evaluation must sign and date the checklist, as does the employee being observed. This documentation must be kept with the employee's education records. When observing a psychomotor skill, use a checklist similar to the one in Figure 21.1.

Competency documentation form

FIGURE 21.1

Demonstration of competency achievement for

_____

Date: _____

Objectives: _____

_____

_____

Competency demonstration:

Step 1: _____

Step 2: _____

Step 3: _____

Step 4: _____

Observer comments: _____

_____

_____

_____

Competency was achieved: _____

Observer's signature

_____

Learner's signature

Competency was not achieved: _____

Observer's signature

The following steps will be taken by the learner to achieve competency:

_____

_____

_____

_____

Learner's signature

Evidence of learning plus the reaction form demonstrates program value to a certain extent. However, an even better way to demonstrate program value is to obtain evidence that the learner actually applied the new knowledge/skill in the work setting.

References

Abdulhadi, L., and Hull, E. (2001). "Program evaluation and return on investment."
    In A. E. Avillion (Ed.) *Core curriculum for staff development*. pp. 343–360.
    Pensacola, FL: The National Nursing Staff Development Organization (NNSDO).

Avillion, A. E. (1998). *The redesign of nursing staff development*. Pensacola, FL: NNSDO.

Chapter 22

Level three: Behavior

This level involves assessing learners' behavior, or the actual use of new knowledge/skills during job performance. This level of evaluation takes more time and effort than the previous two levels.

Using new knowledge/skills requires the support and encouragement of management and administration. Ask yourself, "Do employees, including managers and administrators, understand how new knowledge and skills affect the organization?" To make it easier for learners to take on new behaviors, answer the following questions before education is offered:

- How is job performance to be affected by the new knowledge/skills?

- Has the impact of education been clearly communicated to learners, managers, and administrators?

- Does the work environment facilitate the acquisition and use of new knowledge/skills by providing necessary equipment, staffing, etc.?

How will you evaluate behavior? There are several options including direct observation, review of documentation, and assessing the appropriateness of patient-care interventions. Whichever method you choose, be sure that there is consistency throughout this level. Suppose a new patient treatment modality has recently been implemented at your organization. You have provided appropriate education including rationale for treatment, demonstration and return demonstration of the treatment, and the essential documentation for this technique. Reaction evaluations are positive, and you have determined that learning has taken place. How then do you assess transfer of knowledge to the work setting (i.e., behavior)? Here are some suggestions:

- Review the patient's medical record for accuracy in documenting new procedures and the patient's response

- Check use of any equipment that is part of the treatment modality for accuracy

- Directly observe nurses as they perform the procedure

These examples are all appropriate ways to measure behavior. However, as with steps taken to measure knowledge acquisition, there must be consistency of evaluation among those who observe, review, etc. Develop guidelines for evaluators and take the time to be sure that anyone who acts as an observer understands how to follow such guidelines. Again, a template is a useful time saver. Keep it in your computer and adapt it quickly for your level-three evaluations.

Evaluation of behavior (applied knowledge)

FIGURE 22.1

Date: _____

Time: _____

Objectives: _____

_____

_____

Evaluation procedure

Medical record review: _____

_____

_____

_____

Equipment use: _____

_____

_____

_____

Direct observation: _____

_____

_____

_____

Evaluator's comments _____

_____

_____

_____

_____

Evaluator's signature

References

Avillion, A. E. (1998). *The redesign of nursing staff development.* Pensacola, FL: The National Nursing Staff Development Organization (NNSDO).

Kirkpatrick, D. L. (1998). "Great ideas revisited." In D. L. Kirkpatric (Compiler) *Another look at evaluating training programs* (pp. 3–8). Alexandria, VA: American Society for Training and Development (ASTD).

Chapter 23

Level four: Results/Impact

Learner satisfaction has been positive, knowledge acquisition has been demonstrated, and on-the-job behaviors have changed and indicate application of new knowledge and skills. Good for you! Now your chief executive officer (CEO) wants to know how these results affect the organization.

Level four takes considerable time and effort and is generally done when education programs are intended to help the organization achieve an important goal. Use the data you collected during level three as the foundation for this level of evaluation.

Let's continue with the example from the preceding chapters: Behavioral evaluation indicates that a new treatment modality has been safely and accurately learned by nursing employees who received appropriate training and education. How do you assesses whether these behavior changes benefit the organization? Here are recommendations for the developing a procedure to evaluate the results.

Begin by confirming that knowledge acquisition and knowledge application (behavior) were accurately and consistently evaluated. Asking the following guestions:

- Have the outcomes of patients receiving the new treatment modality improved?

- Have their lengths of stay decreased?

- Is there a decrease in nosocomial infections?

- Did health insurance reimbursement increase as a result of nursing documentation that helps to justify the new treatment?

- Did the successful implementation of this treatment enhance the organization's ability to meet accreditation standards?

- Do performance evaluations indicate an improvement in job performance?

Use the answers to these questions to establish evidence that education contributed to a positively to the organization. Do not work in isolation from other departments. Department/unit managers, members of the research department or research committee, and quality-improvement staff are valuable resources. The data collected as part of this level is important to all of these work areas. By sharing resources and time you and your colleagues can develop a level-four evaluation method that measures impact from a variety of sources.

Presenting your data to leadership

When presenting level-four data, be prepared for those who will challenge you to provide concrete proof that education was directly responsible for positive results. This type of proof is generally impossible to gather. Don't let this deter you from conducting level-four evaluations. You can not be absolutely certain whether behavior changes and corresponding results are because of education or due to another source. However, you can provide evidence that a link exists between education and results by collecting the data previously described. This is another good reason to involve your colleagues in data collection. Your evidence may indicate that education was effective, but also that the actions of managers or others contributed to positive results. Gather allies by explaining how your evaluation process will make them look good, too.

Do not use the word "proof" when presenting your data. It's too easily disputed. To prove an exact cause-and-effect relationship between education and results, you would have to eliminate all other factors that might have influenced behaviors. In a healthcare setting, this is nearly impossible. Use the word "evidence" instead.

Here are more examples of factors that can link education with positive organizational results:

- Decreased staff turnover

- Decreased patient falls

- Decreased medication errors

- Decreased employee injuries

- Decreased employee sick days

- Increase in customer (i.e., patient/family) satisfaction

- Increased profitability

References

Avillion, A. E. (1998). *The redesign of nursing staff development.* Pensacola, FL: The National Nursing Staff Development Organization (NNSDO).

Kirkpatrick, D. L. (1998). "Evaluating training programs: Evidence vs. proof." In D. L. Kirkpatrick (Compiler) *Another look at evaluating training programs.* pp. 9–11. Alexandria, VA: American Society for Training and Development (ASTD).

Kirkpatrick, D. L. (1998). "Great ideas revisited." In D. L. Kirkpatric (Compiler) *Another look at evaluating training programs.* pp. 3–8. Alexandria, VA: ASTD.

Chapter 24

Level five:
Return on investment

The purpose of this level is to demonstrate your education's effect on the department's/ organization's financial bottom line. A return on investment (ROI) calculation requires a cost-benefit analysis. This is a time-consuming process, so perform this analysis only when it is imperative for your department's (or your organization's) survival or when you must demonstrate your financial worth to the organization.

Suppose you have made extensive changes in your new employee-orientation program. Your goal might be to demonstrate that these changes result in decreased turnover, decreased length of orientation, and decreased dollars spent to orient staff.

To begin an ROI study of these education changes, determine the cost of orientation under the old system. Answer the following questions:

- How long did orientation take?

- How much overtime was required to pay employees working extra shifts until new employees were able to safely assume their duties?

- How much staff-development and preceptor time was spent orienting new employees? (Using their hourly wages, determine how much money was paid to staff who did the orienting and to new staff being oriented.)

- How much preparation time did it take to plan orientation programs? (Again, determine costs in salary for this preparation time.)

- How much money did supplies, equipment, etc. used for orientation cost?

- What was the turnover rate for new employees? (Determine how long you want to consider employees as new. Does it mean through probation? Within one year of employment?)

Next, answer these same questions based on the new orientation program. Ideally, you should obtain a year's worth of data. But the hectic pace of the healthcare industry will probably not allow for that much time. Use the length of time that employees are considered new as the appropriate period for data collection. In other words, if you're analyzing the new orientation program for six months, collect six months' of data under the old system.

Calculate ROI as a percentage. Divide the dollar value of the program (net program benefits) by the total cost of the training. Net program befits are the program benefits minus the program costs. The formula looks something like this:

$$ROI\ (\%) = \frac{Net\ program\ benefits}{Program\ costs \times 100}$$

Figure the ROI for both the new and the old orientation programs.

You can also report ROI as a simple dollar amount. Cite how much more it costs to orient new employees under the old system v. the new system in dollars by comparing expenses for such programs. You should be able to give administration a specific amount. Wouldn't it be wonderful to be able to say the new orientation system saves the hospital $25,000 quarterly?

Work with your financial experts to develop sound methods of evaluating ROI. They are accustomed to looking at outcomes in terms of dollars and cents. Not all clinicians or educators have this expertise. Don't be afraid to seek help from your colleagues.

References

Abdulhadi, L., and Hull, E. (2001). "Program evaluation and return on investment."
In Avillion, A.E. (Ed.) *Core curriculum for staff development.* pp. 343–360).
Pensacola, FL: The National Nursing Staff Development Organization (NNSDO).

Avillion, A. E. (1998). *The redesign of nursing staff development.* Pensacola, FL: NNSDO.

Kirkpatrick, D. L. (1998). "Evaluating training programs: Evidence vs. proof."
In D. L. Kirkpatrick (Compiler) *Another look at evaluating training programs.* pp. 9–11.
Alexandria, VA: American Society for Training and Development (ASTD).

Kirkpatrick, D. L. (1998). "Great ideas revisited." In D. L. Kirkpatric (Compiler) *Another look at evaluating training programs.* pp. 3–8. Alexandria, VA: ASTD.

How to use the files on your CD-ROM

The following file names correspond with figures listed in this book.

File name	Document
Fig 2-1.rtf	Sample values statement
Fig 2-2.rtf	Sample vision statement #1
Fig 2-3.rtf	Sample vision statement #2
Fig 2-4.rtf	Recommendations for crafting a vision
Fig 2-5.rtf	Sample mission statement
Fig 2-6.rtf	Characteristics of a mission statement
Fig 2-7.rtf	Sample goal and corresponding objectives
Fig 3-1.rtf	Culture of learning
Fig 6-1.rtf	Implementing adult learning principles
Fig 7-1.rtf	Learning styles cheat sheet
Fig 8-1.rtf	Multigenerational teaching techniques organizer
Fig 9-1.rtf	Diversity education planner
Fig 14-1.rtf	Sample needs assessment form
Fig 17-1.rtf	Inservice documentation form (new policies/regulations)
Fig 17-2.rtf	Inservice documentation form (new equipment)
Fig 20-1.rtf	Classroom evaluation form
Fig 20-2.rtf	Distance-learning evaluation form
Fig 21-1.rtf	Competency documentation form
Fig 22-1.rtf	Evaluation of behavior (applied knowledge)

You will find the following files on the CD-ROM only and not in the book:

Fig 11-1.rtf	Resourceful teaching strategies
Fig 13-1.rtf	Using Benner's framework for program planning

To adapt any of the files to your own facility, simply follow the instructions below to open the CD.

If you have trouble reading the forms, click on "View," and then "Normal." To adapt the forms, save them first to your own hard drive or disk (by clicking "File," then "Save as," and changing the system to your own). Then change the information enclosed in brackets to fit your facility, and add or delete any items that you wish to change.
Installation instructions

This product was designed for the Windows operating system and includes Word files that will run under Windows 95/98 or greater. The CD will work on all PCs and most Macintosh systems. To run the files on the CD-ROM, take the following steps:

1. Insert the CD into your CD-ROM drive.

2. Double-click on the "My Computer" icon, next double-click on the CD drive icon.

3. Double-click on the files you wish to open.

4. Adapt the files by moving the cursor over the areas you wish to change, highlighting them, and typing in the new information using Microsoft Word.

5. To save a file to your facility's system, click on "File" and then click on "Save As." Select the location where you wish to save the file and then click on "Save."

6. To print a document, click on "File" and then click on "Print."

Related products from HcPro

Books

Nurse Preceptor Training System

As your workforce of seasoned RNs dwindles, your ability to successfully train and orient new nurses has a direct effect on retention. Nurse preceptors help guide new nurses through orientation and help them adjust to their new role and work environment. Time-crunched nurse managers need an all-in-one solution to plan, set up, run, and evaluate an effective nurse preceptor training program that is guaranteed to produce exceptional preceptors and competent new nurses every time.

The book, handbook and CD-ROM set, **Nurse Preceptor Training System,** contains every tool a new preceptor needs to turn new nurses or nursing students into competent, energized members of the staff. Applicable to nurses in any setting, this "workshop-in-a-box" resource is your complete guide to successfully implementing a new preceptor training program, or revitalizing your existing program. It will help you retain your new nurses by giving them the best preceptors possible.

Surviving the Nursing Shortage: Strategies for recruitment and retention

Nurses around the country are entering retirement, while multiple factors, including low pay, mandatory overtime, and stressful working conditions cause younger nurses to leave the profession. Meanwhile, fewer young people are pursuing a career in nursing. As a nurse leader, nursing staff recruitment and retention is now your biggest challenge. With the "how-to" strategies, tips, and tools from industry veterans and experts that this book offers, you'll be able to

- attract top nurses to your facility
- retain your current nursing staff and become a "Magnet Manager"

- measure your recruitment and retention progress
- successfully market your hospital in your community
- provide the highest level of patient care possible

Managing Documentation Risk: Tools for nurse managers

Protect yourself and your staff nurses from being named in malpractice lawsuits by making sure your documentation is the best it can be. All nurses—from frontline to executive—need to understand what they are liable for when their nursing care is implicated in legal cases. They also need to learn strategies that will help them protect themselves while still offering the best quality of care.

Managing Documentation Risk: Tools for nurse managers is a comprehensive reference tool all nurses will use to improve nursing documentation and decrease the likelihood of nursing liability related to incomplete or inaccurate documentation. It includes the 160-page book **Managing Documentation Risk: A Guide for Nurse Managers,** as well as 25 copies of **Nursing Documentation: Reduce Your Risk of Liability,** a 32-page training handbook specifically for staff nurses.

Handling Difficult Patients: Management tools for staff preparedness

Nurses across the country are being challenged every day to meet the needs of a sicker and more complex patient population. Difficult patients along with their families demand more nursing time and more facility resources, and can even jeopardize the personal safety of the nursing staff. **Handling Difficult Patients: Management Tools for Staff Preparedness** is an exciting new training package written to help the nursing staff manage difficult patients. The package includes a 150-page book, **Handling Difficult Patients: A Nurse Manager's Guide,** and 25 copies of **Handling Difficult Patients: A Guide for Staff,** the 32-page companion staff training handbook.

Each patient presents the staff with a unique set of issues. This training package is the tool you and your staff need to understand these patient issues and learn how to handle them.

Newsletters

Strategies for Nurse Managers

As a nurse leader, you know first hand how important it is to stay on top of the latest developments in your field. From the JCAHO's 2004 Patient Safety Goals to preparing for bioterrorism, it's virtually impossible to do on your own.

Strategies for Nurse Managers is a 12-page monthly how-to resource that was created exclusively to help you save time performing your job successfully. Each monthly issue provides nurse leaders like you with field-tested ideas, tips, and how-to's on managing effectively, gaining the respect of your peers and employees, recruiting and retaining the best staff, making the best of employee relations, and avoiding the number one pitfall of nurse managers—burnout.

It takes roughly 30 minutes each month to read this newsletter while the rewards last all month!

To obtain additional information, to order the above products, or to comment on *A Practical Guide to Staff Development: Tools and techniques for effective education*, please contact us at:

HCPro, Inc.
P.O. Box 1168
Marblehead, MA 01945

Toll-free telephone: 800/650-6787
Toll-free fax: 800/639-8511
E-mail: customerservice@hcpro.com
Internet: www.hcmarketplace.com